Praise for *Paid to Piss People Off: Book 1 PEACE, Book 2 PORN, Book 3 PRAYER*

"Barry Lynn does it again! This tale of his life and work is every bit as inspiring and energizing as all the hard work he's done so far. You will be entertained and occasionally horrified by the people and institutions he has taken on. He shows how real activism works and how you can do the work too!"

—Thom Hartmann, progressive national radio and television host and best-selling author

"Barry Lynn brilliantly expresses his ideas which he delivers with wit, humor, and panache. If this book is in your hands, you're lucky. Open it and start reading. You'll be glad you did."

—Lewis Black, comedian

"Barry Lynn has been a tenacious advocate for peace and justice. I am glad that he has gotten around to writing this memoir of his extraordinary life."

—Pat Schroeder, former Congresswoman from Colorado

"Barry Lynn has created an important and beautiful literary treasure. Lynn is brilliant and courageous, a key figure in the amnesty and peace movements who has written an unforgettable portrait of a generation in turmoil. This is a fascinating history lesson told with wit, honesty, and grace."

—Ron Kovic, Vietnam veteran and author of *Born on the Fourth of July*

"Barry Lynn is a national treasure and *Paid to Piss People Off* perfectly captures his trajectory. He built a career out of poking holes in hypocrisy and religious zealotry using an artful blend of substance, humor, and incisive wit. This book captures the unvarnished essence of the Rev. Barry Lynn, one of the most important voices of his generation."

—Wade Henderson, former President of the Leadership Conference on Civil and Human Rights

"Lucky Barry Lynn for leading such a fun life. And lucky for all of us for him to have led such a purposeful life. Decades of work on civil rights, peace, and true religious freedom make me proud to be one of his fellow travelers."

—Bill Press, former co-host of CNN's Crossfire and award-winning author

"Barry Lynn is one of the rare people who recognize the deep connection between social justice, music, comedy, and film. He understands and never waivers in his support of folks on the margins of society. I think he likes us more than the powerful politicians he has worked with all these years. Barry is a gem; his words, truth to power. These three volumes are thrilling."

—Mary Gauthier, Grammy nominated songwriter and
author of *Saved by A Song*

"I observed Barry Lynn doing the difficult dance between faith and social policy for three decades, regretfully mainly as his ideological nemesis. Too late in life I concluded that he was mostly right and I was mostly wrong. This memoir helps me make up for lost time and might allow others to do the same."

—The Rev. Rob Schenck, director of the
Bonhoeffer Institute and former leader
in the anti-abortion movement

"Barry Lynn has always been a powerful speaker and leader of progressive causes, and a strong advocate for women's privacy and bodily integrity. This book is a clarion call to the next generations to never give up on fighting hard for what is right."

—Kim Gandy, Past President of the National Organization
for Women and current President of the National
Network to End Domestic Violence.

Paid to Piss People Off:
Book 2 PORN

Barry W. Lynn

Blue Cedar Press
Wichita, Kansas

Paid to Piss People Off: Book 2, PORN

Copyright © 2023 Red Toad Books LLC

All rights reserved. No part of this book may be reproduced in any form or by any electronic or mechanical means, including information storage and retrieval systems, without permission in writing from the publisher except for brief quotations in critical articles and reviews. Inquiries should be addressed to:

Blue Cedar Press
P.O. Box 48715
Wichita, KS 67201

Visit the Blue Cedar Press website: *www.bluecedarpress.com*

10 9 8 7 6 5 4 3 2 1
First edition April 2023
ISBN: 978-1-958728-10-9 (paper)
ISBN: 978-1-958728-12-3 (ebook)

Cover design by Barry W. Lynn, Joanne Lynn, and Gina Laiso.
Cover photo: Edwin Meese, Attorney General, receiving Porn
   Commission Report. Associated Press.
Interior design by Gina Laiso, Integrita Productions.
Editors Laura Tillem and Gretchen Eick.

Library of Congress Control Number (LCCN): 2023931759

Printed in the United States of America

Note: Images are from Author's personal collection unless otherwise identified.

TABLE OF CONTENTS

INTRODUCTION

In Washington, DC, hundreds of Davids try to slay Goliaths, Goliaths such as: "the military-industrial complex" President Eisenhower warned the nation about when his terms as president ended. Or Big Pharma and the insurance industry that keep health care costs in the U.S. the highest in the world. Or "Dark Money" that since the 2006 *Citizens United* Supreme Court decision has allowed billionaires to sway our elections. Consider the prison industrial complex that has made the U.S. the biggest jailer in the world. Or the Religious Right and its allies in Congress waging their "culture wars" against public schools and concepts of human rights.

Davids exhaust themselves hurling their stones at giants. Usually they burn out and move to other careers. Barry W. Lynn would not burn out. From the 1970s to the 2010s he used his lawyer skills, his keen mind and devastating wit, and his pastoral empathy against the Goliaths. He aimed his smooth stones at those who would punish young people who refused to kill others in war (Book 1), at those who would withhold rights protected in the First Amendment of the U.S. Constitution (Book 2), and at the Religious Right that sought to erase the Constitution's core principle of the separation of church and state (Book 3).

His stones were his keen legal arguments and he delivered them with sharp humor. That made him a popular speaker at press conferences and hearings, on television and radio and podcasts. This is his story. It includes politicians and activists, as well as the comedians, musicians, actors, and movies that kept him sane as he persisted. Lynn's phenomenal ability to keep engaging in debate and conversation with leaders of those Goliaths, entering their spaces to listen to them and take them on, makes his story an entertaining and educational tour of the last five decades.

Blue Cedar Press

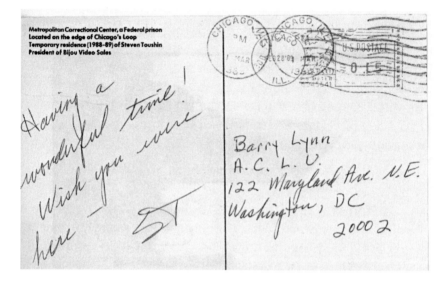

Metropolitan Correctional Center, a Federal prison
Located on the edge of Chicago's Loop
Temporary residence (1988-89) of Steven Toushin
President of Bijou Video Sales

Having a
wonderful time!
Wish you were
here __

Barry Lynn
A. C. L. U.
122 Maryland Ave. N.E.
Washington, DC
            20002

Toushin was incarcerated for distribution of gay pornography.
He clearly had a sense of humor.

Chapter 1

DEFENDING THE FIRST AMENDMENT FOR THE ACLU

I have supported the American Civil Liberties Union since I sent that letter to them when I was in high school, thanking them for their clear opposition to the Vietnam War on constitutional grounds. However, I never dreamed of actually working for them. This was another "dream job" that came to pass.

Sometimes working for a high-powered bureaucrat in Washington brings unexpected challenges and leads to a new career. That was the case for Mort Halperin who worked for Dr. Henry Kissinger in the late Sixties but resigned in 1970 when his telephone was wiretapped. He sued Kissinger, successfully. The American Civil Liberties Union (ACLU) hired him to work on matters of national security, particularly to address balancing legitimate needs to protect secrets with the right of the public to see information they need to make informed decisions. Halperin created the Center for National Security Studies, with analysts including Robert Borosage.

After John Shattuck left his position as Director of the ACLU's office in Washington to go to the JFK Library in Boston, a national search for his replacement ensued. Mort was in the mix, joined most prominently by civil rights icon Julian Bond. Many who knew Mort believed he was the best choice for the job, notwithstanding Bond's history and credentials. Mort did not seek the limelight and rarely appeared as an ACLU voice on television. He often gave his staff these opportunities, including testifying before Congress on ACLU concerns. He preferred to review the testimony of his junior colleagues and give them visibility. "There is nothing you can't get done in Washington if you don't need to take credit for it," he told his staff.

While the ACLU was searching for a director of the Washington office, I was in a kind of employment limbo. I had been hired by the previous director on a temporary basis to deal with church/state matters and censorship. I was to fill in for my close anti-draft colleague David Landau, who had been doing volunteer work for the Presidential campaign of Colorado Senator Gary Hart. While having a midafternoon sandwich with David at a local greasy spoon, he confided that many on the Hart campaign staff were concerned about rumors of Hart's extramarital activities.

This was an era when the press generally didn't pry into the private lives of politicians, except when a stripper/mistress turned up in the Reflecting Pool of the Jefferson Memorial and ended the career of powerful Congressman Wilbur Mills. The incident did briefly upgrade the career of Fannie Foxx, the "Argentina Firecracker."

Hart himself had invited the press to examine his life and look for affairs, almost guaranteeing that his relationship with Donna Rice would eventually be discovered. Many people will remember the notorious photograph showing Rice sitting on Hart's lap aboard a boat called *Monkey Business*.

If those rumors of an affair were true, the Hart campaign could fizzle and burn, David would be back at the ACLU, and I'd be looking for a job.

Hart's campaign did come to a crashing halt, but David decided to take a run at a Congressional seat. Unfortunately, he lost, although he is still active in high-level Pennsylvania politics.

Filling in for David in 1984 did not come with an expectation that I would be offered a permanent position. However, my ACLU colleagues were very encouraging. When Mort was finally selected to lead the ACLU Washington office, he offered me a full-time position working on religious freedom, censorship, and, for a brief time, the AIDS crisis.

Mort taught me and others how to manage a staff. Many of the folks in that office went on to take management positions when they left the ACLU. Jerry Berman, then in the process of becoming a leading national expert on computers and civil liberties, moved to manage the Electronic Freedom Foundation. Leslie Harris moved to the Center for Democracy and Technology, Diann Rust-Tierney to the National Coalition to Abolish the Death Penalty, and Wade Henderson to the NAACP and then the Leadership Conference on Civil and Human Rights.

The ACLU had a family atmosphere, with only occasional intra-family disputes. Mine was a fuss with Leslie over moving to a nicer office and the meaning of seniority, which Mort ultimately resolved in my favor. Leslie accepted the decision, and we are still friends because Mort tried to resolve disagreements with equity, rationality, and fundamental decency.

Mort and I had minor policy differences over religious matters and the policies surrounding them. He initially thought that the bill to provide rooms for student religious clubs to meet in public high schools was acceptable, while I thought it needed to be defeated unless it contained a right for *all* student clubs to meet. Eventually, that change was made, but many ACLU members felt that accommodating religious clubs was qualitatively different from accommodating other clubs.

My First Religious Practice Issue

My assignment was protecting the freedom to practice your religion that is guaranteed in the Bill of Rights, First Amendment, in a way that does not result in favoring a particular religion.

My first exposure to this constellation of issues came when the U.S. Supreme Court issued the decision *Employment Division v. Smith* in 1990. In *Employment Division v. Smith,* a majority of the Court, led by Justice Scalia, had ruled that two Native American drug counselors could be fired by the State of Oregon when they were found to be using a somewhat hallucinogenic cactus called peyote in a religious ritual. They had claimed that, although peyote was unlawful for others, they as Native Americans had a right to not be penalized for its use for their religious purposes. Peyote use in Native American religious practices had been contested since the beginning of the twentieth century. The Court majority disagreed, Scalia claiming that such exemptions would be akin to "anarchy" with "a system in which each conscience is a law unto itself."

Mort attended a meeting with Senators Ted Kennedy (D/MA) and Orrin Hatch (R/UT) the day after the Court decision to discuss how Congress could correct/reverse the decision through legislation. Both conservative and progressive religious groups feared that this was setting a new and lower standard for claims under the First Amendment's protection of "free exercise of religion." They argued that a legislative fix was warranted. I had mixed feelings about where any legislation might lead, and Mort took to heart my concerns about the possible consequences of legislation. During that meeting, he got commitments from Senator Orrin Hatch (R/UT) that no bill could be used to support claims of religious school "voucher" advocates, even though Hatch himself supported vouchers. The bill was seen as a way to permit Sikh firefighters to wear turbans, certain religious prisoners to grow beards, and possibly to allow exceptions to drug laws for use in religious rituals, though conservatives were loath to mention this. There were hearings and much conversation about this legislative fix, but between 1990 and 1994 the proposal languished in committee.

Eventually the bill passed, having minimal effect initially. It was declared partly unconstitutional on the grounds that it preempted state law. Later the bill re-emerged as a weapon against coverage of birth control in the Affordable Care Act (ACA). In the lengthy debates on the ACA in the House and Senate, no one suggested this wording would be used to allow institutions to deny coverage of birth control. If someone had told Senator Kennedy that this legislation would be used by institutions to avoid providing women birth control, I am convinced there never would have been a bill in the first place. All these years later, for-profit corporations can deny their female employees the right to birth control coverage, due to the 2014 Supreme Court ruling in *Burwell v. Hobby Lobby*.

The Start of the Meese Pornography Commission

Another part of my First Amendment rights portfolio was protecting freedom of speech. Pornography may represent the end of human civilization, or a harmless fantasy, but you can be assured that any government body investigating pornography will not take the issue seriously, only being concerned with political fallout. Exhibit

One: Ronald Reagan's decision in 1984 to set up a Commission on this topic under the auspices of then-Attorney General William French Smith. The Pornography Commission extended into Edwin Meese's tenure as Attorney General and is known as The Meese Commission.

I knew this creature was coming and lobbied extensively to track it on behalf of the ACLU. I think the ACLU hierarchy believed I as a clergyman might be more effective. I knew I would be aided greatly by Isabelle Katz Pinzler, the highly regarded head of the Women's Rights Project, which had earlier been led by Ruth Bader Ginsburg. In that capacity I would be the Commission's major nemesis.

Reagan himself had called for the establishment of this study group to assess vague "new evidence," allegedly accumulated since an earlier 1970 federal study of pornography had found no link between sexually explicit material and any forms of anti-social behavior. Any doubt about Reagan's group's objectivity was erased when the official "notice of establishment" of the new commission was published in *The Federal Register* and labeled pornography a "serious national problem," study of which was essential to "reflect the concern a healthy society must have regarding the ways in which its people entertain themselves." The goal was to find "more effective ways in which the spread of pornography could be curtailed." In other words, the Commission was not directed to consider if this expression of sexuality was a problem, but just find ways to suppress an assumed problem.

The composition of this eleven-member body similarly left no doubt about its intention. The Chair was Henry Hudson, the Commonwealth's Attorney for Arlington County, Virginia, just outside Washington, DC. He had started a crusade the previous year to eliminate all "adult businesses" in that jurisdiction, including forcing video stores to rid themselves of any adult films in their inventory and convincing local convenience stores to stop selling *Playboy* and *Penthouse* magazines. Here are the rest of the members.

James Dobson was President of Focus on The Family and later creator of the lobbying offshoot, still extremely active today, the Family Research Council—labeled a hate group by the Southern Poverty Law Center. His innocuous daily commentaries on family life were run on virtually all CBS-affiliated radio stations in the United States. Most listeners had never heard the hard-edged screeds he delivered in other religious venues about the dangers of "liberal attitudes," including what he called the "Playboy lifestyle."

Father Bruce Ritter, founder of Covenant House, a shelter for runaway youth then operating solely off Times Square in New York City, had initiated an assault on pornography in 1979. By 1984, he had created and distributed a lengthy article that asserted that children were being exposed to "explicit pornography" on cable television in their homes, that "legally obscene" pornography materials were being sold in over 20,000 bookstores in America, and that "organized crime" was deeply involved in the distribution of this material.

Harold "Tex" Lazar, who wore cowboy boots to most meetings, was well known in conservative circles. Lazar had worked as a speechwriter for William F. Buckley, Jr., Richard Nixon, and Attorney General Smith. Indeed, he was instrumental in convincing Smith to set up the Commission in the first place. Wasting no time, within a few months of the Commission's start, he sent fellow Commissioners a long letter detailing all manner of new law enforcement efforts he felt should be undertaken against smut.

Judge Edward Garcia, a Reagan-appointed federal district court judge in California, had been a county prosecutor who regularly brought obscenity cases. As a local Sacramento County, California, judge, he regularly sentenced people on obscenity charges, unusual in the state. In a business meeting of the Commission in Chicago in July of 1985, he expressed surprise that some of the material shown to the Commission was "masochistic." That told me that whatever he had been sentencing people for in his court was far tamer material.

Diane Cusack was the vice-mayor of Scottsdale, Arizona, and used restrictive zoning and regulation of "public dancing" to curtail adult businesses there. She told a group of anti-pornography advocates that they should photograph customers and record license plate numbers of patrons of an adult theater in order to drive the theater out of business by shaming its customers.

Frederick Schauer was a law professor at the University of Michigan who wrote in a law journal that pornography was entitled to no First Amendment protection because the "prototypical pornographic item on closer analysis shares more of the characteristics of sexual activity than of the communicative process." In other words, it is not "speech" but more analogous to a dildo or a visit to a prostitute.

Park E. Dietz was both a sociologist and psychiatrist at the University of Virginia Law School. He studied pornography and "detective magazines" which depicted women in distress on their lurid covers. He claimed that "sadism and masochism... play a role in all pornography" and concluded that young men can develop sexual disorders if they masturbate to particular images involving "deviant" or criminal behavior.

The other three members (all women) had no known preconceptions regarding pornography: **Ellen Levine,** editor of *Woman's Day*; **Deanne Tilton,** a Commissioner on the California Attorney General's Commission on the Enforcement of Child Abuse Laws; and **Dr. Judith Becker,** a Columbia University clinical psychologist who had counseled extensively with both rape victims and rapists.

The Executive Director of the Commission was **Alan Sears,** chief of the Criminal Division of the U.S. Attorney's Office in Western Kentucky. Sears was one of the only active federal prosecutors of pornography that depicted adults, during the years preceding the creation of the Commission.

With much of this known to me on the day of the formation announcement June 20, 1985, I told *The New York Times* (in what would become the Quote of the Day), "I believe that a train marked 'censorship' has just left the station." That line began the war between me and the chairman of the Commission, **Henry Hudson.**

Lynn issues an ACLU response to the Commission's launch of a campaign against pornography. Source: Getty Images.

The Porn Commission Gets Underway

The first formal hearing occurred over two days in late June in Washington, DC. I testified for the ACLU and listened to hours of commentary by others. Before lunch on the first day, I knew my original negative view of the Commission might have been understated. However, the turnout of press for that event was so great that I knew that this would be a royal opportunity to garner attention if I could just establish that I was either smarter or better looking than other possible critics. Maybe I should just keep up the level of smart-ass quotes I used like the "train marked censorship" line.

I testified with Isabelle Katz Pinzler on the afternoon of the second day of hearings in Washington, indicating that I feared that the Commission would embrace "moral mob rule," saying, "The First Amendment may not be suspended because an image or idea causes the most susceptible or malleable person who hears it or sees it to behave in an antisocial manner." I also made two other central points. First, the country should not treat words or pictures about sexuality any differently from similar material about any other topic, since all words and images communicate ideas, albeit often ideas that some consider reprehensible in the case of pornography. Indeed, if the ideas were not there, there would be little reason for pro-censorship forces to object to them on religious or political grounds. Second, the legal construct of "obscenity" was so broad and vague as to create a "chilling effect" on speech. The so-called "Miller test" to determine if an item was obscene was developed by the Supreme Court in 1973. It asked whether "the average person, applying contemporary community standards" would find that the work taken as a whole, "appeals to the prurient interest...depicts or describes in a patently offensive way, sexual conduct specifically defined by... applicable state law" and "lacks serious literary, artistic, political or scientific value." If an item meets these standards, it is by definition "obscene."

Hudson went on to badger Isabelle about whether the ACLU had ever received funding from the Playboy Foundation. She indicated that it had but categorically rejected his implication that any funding had influenced our position, stating unequivocally "We don't accept grants with strings." I continued by noting that this "off handed comment does not serve the Commission well...it is totally inappropriate." Hudson retorted, "Your observation, too, is noted."

Those first two days of testimony had parallels in most of the subsequent meetings: politicians addressing the moral decadence of porn, slide shows by anti-pornography law enforcement officials (as if searching for the single most disgusting and repulsive image ever created would prove that all sexual material should be suppressed), testimony by persons claiming to be victimized by porn (sometimes testifying behind curtains), and curious factoids to "prove" the danger of pornography.

In that first Washington DC hearing, the politicians who discussed the immorality of porn included Senators Mitch McConnell (R/KY) (yes, he was there even then) and Alabama's Jeremiah Denton (R/AL). FBI agent Ken Lanning presented a most detailed slide show, clicking through photos from *Erotica Grotesque* magazine picturing sex with canines and chickens and scrotum piercings. One of the "victims" of porn was a spouse named Sharon whose husband was so obsessed with porn that all of his criticism of her was based on her alleged sexual failings, "If I burned the toast, he said it was because I was frigid." On the factoid front, a witness indicated that virtually every person found to possess "child pornography" also had a copy of the advertisement for Coppertone suntan lotion that featured a little girl having the bottom of her swimsuit pulled partially down by a small dog. Many of us thought this just shows that if you are inclined to get sexually aroused by children, even the most harmless image could serve that purpose. Among the "harms" of pornography was a description of the damage done by masturbating with a vacuum cleaner. Politicians continued reciting tales of immorality, slideshows of horror, "victim" testimony, and strange facts at the subsequent hearings in Los Angeles, Miami, Chicago, Houston, and New York City.

Henry Hudson had what turned out to be a very bad public relations strategy, and I was happy to exploit it. The Commission was established as a Federal Advisory Commission, a status that included quite rigid rules, including a statutory requirement that all materials produced for the Commission would be available to the public as soon as they were sent to Commissioners. Hudson also got the members to agree that there would be no public statement until the Final Report was issued. This gave me the opportunity to get access to all their materials, disseminate them to reporters on the First Amendment beat, comment on those materials, and then have Hudson say he couldn't discuss anything until the end of the process.

Here is an early example of how my access to materials played out. At an early meeting, the Commission discussed "rubber goods" like vibrators and dildos. Tentatively, they were leaning toward calling for a complete national ban on such items. As the material was being produced for a final vote on this matter, I got it and sent it to Phil Shenon of the *New York Times* and Howard Kurtz of *The Washington Post*. The next day headline in the *Post* was "Porn Commission

Considers National Ban on Sex Toys." It seemed so goofy that this proposal was essentially dead.

Along the way, only a few journalists were intensely interested in this process aside from Shenon and Kurtz. One was Bob Scheer of *The Los Angeles Times* (who also wrote occasionally for *Playboy*). I had read Bob's reporting in the magazine *Ramparts*, an early journalistic opponent of the Vietnam War and the first and possibly only American magazine investigated by the Central Intelligence Agency for possible Communist ties. The other journalists who followed the Commission's progress included the team of Philip Nobile and Eric Nadler, who were on the payroll of several of Bob Guccione's publications including *Penthouse Forum*. They later co-authored the very detailed book, *United States of America vs. Sex*.

Nobile and Nadler were very different people. Nobile had been a hot-shot editor at *New York Magazine* whose career never quite recovered from their firing him. At one dinner I had with him and several women staffers at *Penthouse*, he leaned over and whispered in my ear, "I've only slept with one of these women. Guess who it is."

By contrast, Nadler was a leftist, deeply interested in South African politics and a family man, now with a new child. Conversations with him were more likely to be about taking children to the zoo than sleeping around with office colleagues. I figured prominently in their reporting on the Commission. At one point, they referred to me as "telegenic." I assume they meant that I could come up with snappy sound bites and argue lucidly on television, not that people would switch off David Hasselhoff or Kevin Costner to see if they could leer at me on another channel. I surmised that my appearing on television at least wouldn't scare children or pets from the room.

I would walk over to the Commission's office, about ten blocks from the ACLU office, and get those materials within hours of them being sent to the Commissioners. Then, I could disseminate them to the journalists I knew were interested but might have to wait days for their mailings from Washington.

In late February 1985, I issued a report for the ACLU called "Rushing to Censorship." The document got considerable attention and enraged many Commission members and right-wing media outlets. Cliff Kincaid, a writer for *Human Events,* reported on how the media "covered up" the nefarious agenda of the ACLU by helping my report "make headlines." He also noted that he attended the press conference at which I released this report by "opening it in a strange manner," noting that I had recently told *Penthouse Forum* magazine that my only complaint was that I wished they hadn't put my interview so close to the article, 'I Had Sex at A Voodoo Orgy.'" Kincaid didn't get the joke.

"Rushing to Censorship" focused on the Commission's six major procedural and analytical "deficiencies." The Commission heard from heavily skewed witness lists and scheduled pro-censorship witnesses early in the day when press interest was highest. The Commission offered friendly treatment to women who claimed negative experiences with adult magazines. For example, ex-Playmate Miki Garcia accused Hugh Hefner of rape and attempted murder and the Commission made no attempt to find supporting evidence. On the other hand, those reporting positive experiences working in the industry were quizzed. Ex-Penthouse Pet Dottie Meyer was questioned by Dietz about comments in the captions that were included in her centerfold, for example, "I like my men rough and tumble living on the edge." She noted sarcastically, "I married a policeman."

Although the Commission expressed an interest in hearing from the pornography industry during its foray to Los Angeles in 1985, only a few lawyers showed up. The city was then trying to use prostitution laws to criminally charge actresses in adult films under the theory they were being paid for "sex" not "acting." Since the Commission could not grant them immunity from such prosecution, it's hardly surprising that these actresses would not show up. A similar claim of interest in "consumers" of pornography drew only two people who might be in that category, again with quite understandable reluctance to discuss their reading habits with a group of people who were on a panel which assumed those interests were a "national problem."

My second gripe was the inordinate focus on searching for images of "aberrant" sexual practices in pornography. Ironically, its only piece of original "research" examined changes in porn since the 1970 report. It created a lengthy slideshow of random centerfolds from *Playboy*, *Penthouse,* and *Hustler* over time. Other than the end of the strategically placed towel in the early Sixties and the apparent discovery of female pubic hair by the early Seventies, not one showed violence or anything that could be called "aberrant" behavior, unless one slide of a *Playboy* model lying in a hammock while holding up a small white dog was seen as some subliminal endorsement of bestiality. Again, these "facts" seemed to help disprove the very point they claimed to be making.

My critique continued with a section on how they could not seem to define the universe of materials they were considering suppressing. At that time, they had tentatively chosen "any representation... which is designed to be sexually arousing and portrays children, pain, humiliation or sexual abuse, conduct or organs as a dominant theme." This sloppy definition did not stop the Commission from coming up with dozens of new enforcement techniques, including mandatory prison sentences, broad forfeiture of all materials in a store if it profited from the sale of even one item deemed "obscene," and removing doors from film booths in "adult stores."

My analysis rejected the Commission's willingness to label as "empirical" social science data linking porn to "harm," while ignoring any data to the contrary. The Commission also would not consider "other aspects of our collective lives and experience" that could bear on the issue. It rejected any effort to judge the credibility of witnesses, with Hudson noting, "I don't believe that type of analysis is necessary. I think it's going to become apparent in how you [the Commission] vote on the factual issues."

The Commission returned frequently to trying to make more material into "child pornography," even arguing that if an image (remember the Coppertone ad?) was used to seduce a child into sexual activity, it should be prosecuted. They characterized cartoons, like one where a grown woman is wearing pigtails, as "child pornography" and urged that allowing children access to any sexually oriented material on cable television should be a new federal crime.

My final criticism was that the Commission was using a circular argument to define how organized crime was involved in pornography. They claimed that anything used to distribute "obscene" material is "organized"—whether it is distributed from a warehouse, transported by a fleet of trucks, or sold via a telephone number. Of course, if there was no "obscenity law" there would be no "crime" to organize around, would there?

I enjoyed an event held just prior to the New York City hearing by the National Coalition Against Censorship. I shared a morning presentation with two of my literary heroes: Betty Friedan and Kurt Vonnegut, Jr. Ms. Friedan, whose seminal work *The Feminine Mystique* was a major force in the creation of the modern feminist movement, discussed how that work was censored and labeled obscene:

If the antipornography legislation, the suppression of pornography was passed, the first targets of it would be feminist books, would be books like Our Bodies Ourselves, *would be books giving women control of their own bodies. The forces behind the antipornography legislation are those that would take away the right of a woman to decide when and whether and how many times to bear a child...They are the very forces that would even suppress books that show women in nontraditional roles, as astronauts or vice presidents or doctors and lawyers. We have to ask, what are they up to in this sideshow, this circus about suppressing pornography?*

Vonnegut gave a memorable sardonic presentation in which he noted, "I make my living with words, and I am ashamed. In view of the terrible damage freely circulated ideas can do to a society, and particularly to innocent children, I beg the government to delete from my works all thoughts that might be dangerous." He continued by quoting the First Amendment, labeling it a "Godless loop of disgusting sexuality," and inquiring, "How could this have happened? Some communistic, pederastic, wife-beating Congressman, while we weren't watching, must have tacked it onto the Rivers and Harbors Bill."

My own presentation summarized much of the criticisms from Rushing to Censorship and concluded, "Last May, when this Commission was announced, I indicated to the press that I feared a train marked censorship had left the Washington station. It has now gotten to about Colorado and hasn't left the track." When I was finished, Vonnegut came up to me and said, "You are a very good writer." This was an extraordinary compliment for which I thanked him, replying, "Maybe I am just a good speaker."

This event continued over lunch and beyond and featured sex educators, social scientists, and actress Colleen Dewhurst, who read from some censored plays. She wrapped it up with the demand, "The government should not have the power to rule art." When the presentations were over, the floor was opened to questions and comments. Adult film star Gloria Leonard quite properly bemoaned that no one at the event represented the "adult entertainment industry" and that perhaps the National Coalition Against Censorship was engaged in "a bit of censorship of its own."

Scandals, Strategies, and Scenes from the Commission

By March of 1986, the Reagan Administration's Justice Department had another embarrassing porn related matter to deal with. Alfred S. Regnery, a Justice Department employee with funding authority over the Commission, was forced to concede that a $734,371 study by "researcher" Judith Reisman, a former producer of the *Captain Kangaroo* television show, was not financially justified. She was paid this money to review 6,004 images of how "children are portrayed in the cartoons and photos of *Playboy, Penthouse*, and *Hustler*." Regnery claimed he had gotten "bad advice from staff" about the grant which was nearly 150% of the budget of the entire Commission. Another controversy resurfaced about an incident ten years earlier in which his wife alleged she had been sexually assaulted by someone seeking to derail her husband's campaign for district attorney. Substantial amounts of pornography and a cache of sex toys were reportedly found in their home. When the story was revisited by Murray Waas of *The New Republic*, Regnery admitted that he had some pornography like "lots of people do." Shortly before the article was published, he resigned from the Reagan Administration. Hypocrisy had finally reached a limit.

Methodist minister the Reverend Donald Wildmon also testified in Los Angeles. In 1976, he formed the National Federation for Decency, later to become the American Family Association. He had felt compelled to turn off the television he was watching with his family during the Christmas holidays when, while flipping channels, he found a scene involving adultery, heard the phrase "son of a bitch," and watched a tied down man being beaten with a hammer.

23

He decided to do something more than turn off the set and formed an organization to force television networks to clean up their acts. Joining forces with the Reverend Jerry Falwell, they created another organization called the Coalition for Better Television (CBTV) and enlisted the support of other organizations. He claimed more than 200 supporting organizations; but *The New York Times Magazine,* in an exhaustive look at Wildmon for a cover story about him, found that CBS News reported that at least one-third of those groups disavowed any connection to CBTV. The monthly publication not only took aim at X-rated films, it chronicled its reflections on every mainstream film and made observations about any television programming it found offensive for any reason. For example, *Charlie's Angels* was too "jiggly"; *The Golden Girls* was "a geriatric sex series."

I believe my first encounter with Wildmon pre-dated the Meese Commission, when he was beginning to battle rock music as well as network television. On a PBS broadcast we debated the topic and Wildmon repeatedly referred to Frank Zappa as a band. It made me happy to hear from a close friend of Zappa say that Zappa was a fan of mine. Most of my connections to Wildmon, though, were directly related to the Meese Commission, in which he also played a significant role. In just one decade after starting his CBTV campaign, Wildmon went from being a small-town Methodist minister to being a panelist on *Meet the Press* and a temporary character in the Pulitzer Prize winning comic strip *Bloom County*, in dialogue with Opus the Penguin.

Henry Hudson, Don Wildmon, Lynn about to appear on Meet the Press.

In October 1985, the Commission met for several days in Los Angeles. Wildmon's principal point in his testimony was that the Commission could do more good by focusing less on sleazy bookstores and more on the mainstream purveyors of porn, including the drug and grocery stores that sold adult magazines, hotel chains that allowed guests to rent unsavory sex-saturated films in their rooms (such as the Ramada Inn), corporate conglomerates that had any, even remote, connection to the materials he considered so dangerous (such as Coca-Cola in Australia), and the major media companies that featured explicit programming through their affiliates. For example, Time, Inc. had an outlet that aired a program called *Hollywood Hot Tubs*. This testimony began a series of events that regurgitated prudish observations and revealed that most of the Commissioners had a disquieting understanding of our judicial system.

Copies of Wildmon's testimony (without his name identified) were sent on Department of Justice stationery to the authorized representatives of all the companies he named. In the key sentence, the cover letter indicated that "The Commission has determined that it would be appropriate to allow your company an opportunity to respond prior to drafting its final report section on identified distributors." It was clear that the report was going to finalize a list of major companies as pornographers, absent adequate rebuttal by those company executives. Within weeks of the receipt of those letters, the Southland Corporation (parent of 7-11 convenience stores) announced that they would no longer carry *Playboy*, *Penthouse*, or *Forum* magazine but denied that the removal was the result of the contact from the Justice Department. Other companies shortly followed suit. Curiously, Southland almost simultaneously instituted a video rental program featuring such titles as *Bloodsucking Freaks* (about a Manhattan torture show) and *Last House on the Left* (containing an oral castration of a rapist by the victim's mother). A philosophy seemed to be developing that bare breasts are bad unless they are being gouged by a machete.

Although Wildmon regularly rejected being labeled a "censor," he was always quick to claim that he was the victim of censorship, even holding a press conference to complain that he wasn't given sufficient credit for presenting his corporate porn testimony to the Commission.

This was technically true because there was no reference to him in the letter to corporate executives from the Commission's Executive Director, Alan Sears. Later, Sears claimed that Wildmon's name was kept out because other people had made similar charges, although I could never find any such references. Wildmon also had a knack for calling all manner of simple corporate decisions "censorship"—much like the claims of "cancel culture" which emerged again in 2020. He even blamed *The Wall Street Journal* for refusing to run an ad for its competitor *USA TODAY* that contained the claim that it sold more daily copies than the *Journal*. I once asked him if his own "decency" newsletter should be required to publish dildo advertisements.

Hudson became so enraged by my constant release of Commission documents with my annotations that he eventually decided, following the meeting in Los Angeles, that, notwithstanding the rules of the Federal Advisory Commission Act, he would not give me any more materials in advance. The word came to me through Alan Sears following a Commission lunch meeting. As an ACLU lawyer, what could I say but, "We will sue you." Sears claimed that the need to restrict distribution of this material was because "organized crime figures" might learn what was being considered. This was preposterous considering that the entire set of hearings on crime had been held openly in New York City just two months earlier. I wrote a letter to Sears: "I know many members of the Commission would like to cover up pornography but that is no reason for the Commission to operate behind a brown paper wrapper." The ACLU also immediately became the client of Patti Goldman, attorney with a Ralph Nader-founded organization called Public Citizen. Our lawsuit announcement was made at a noisy press conference where Ms. Goldman suggested I "refresh" some of my comments from the letter. I did. "This Commission is so obsessed with restricting what other people can see and read about sex that they have now started to censor their own writings on the topic." It was a matter of just five days before the Commission relented and began providing me with all their material again. By this time, I was so annoyed by the Commission's conduct that I issued a statement about how this was "a total capitulation on the part of a corrupt entity." One of the other lawyers at the ACLU office came by and told me I was "burning the bridges by not cutting them any slack." Yup, Burn, baby, burn it was.

The most colorful experiences came from its sojourn in Houston, Texas. Not only was there a business meeting and a hearing, but also, as noted in *The Federal Register*, a field trip to visit adult businesses.

As the sun was setting one evening, the Commission, including one Commissioner's former Hollywood actress wife, who dressed in a gold lame dress for the occasion, and two members of the public, myself, and the prolific feminist writer on "sex panics," Columbia University professor Carole Vance, were on a bus for a field trip to three Houston adult stores. I wrote a long article about this trip but couldn't get it published in *The Nation,* though I had written for them in the past. However, when *The Harvard Civil Rights and Civil Liberties Law Review* reached out for me to write an article and agreed to have students do all the footnoting, it was a lovely opportunity to get my first law review article published and to add the "Houston porn store" article as an addendum.

Two parts of this trip were most bizarre. These stores were sleazy places, one with water from a leaking pipe running over the floor. They could not be mistaken for the "adult stores" now found in many suburban shopping centers, with bright lights and the dildos all lined up against the wall by size and color. At this point in my career, I always wore a coat and tie and looked a lot like the male members of the Commission. At the first store, which had been cased by local police in advance of our arrival, an undercover officer announced after we had been there for a few minutes, "We have two men in this booth engaged in illegal sexual activity." I asked the policeman, "What are we going to do with them?" Since he would have had no idea who I was and I was dressed like everyone else, he probably assumed I was on the Commission. Thus, he said, "We will just let them go home this time because all you folks are here." He had undoubtedly been cautioned that no embarrassing incidents should occur while Reagan officials were present.

The third store was where my single greatest moment of enjoyment shadowing the Commission occurred. I found myself in a "buddy booth" where two or three people could watch a loop of film and perhaps act on their reactions. I found myself in a booth with Chair Henry Hudson and *Woman's Day* editor Ellen Levine. We were observing a film in which two gay men wearing green rubber monster masks were having a sexual encounter. Hudson asked, "So, Barry when you testified before the Commission, you said all these films have meanings. So, what is the meaning of this?" When I responded, "Try it—you might like it," Ms. Levine (already souring on being a part of this Commission) could barely contain her laughter.

In late May, *The Washington Post* published a lengthy article on its Federal Page called "Scientists Say Report Misrepresents Their Findings to Support Conclusions on Sex Violence." Two prominent researchers who had testified were objecting to use of their work in some of the Commission's conclusions. Edward Donnerstein, who had testified in the Houston hearing, complained mightily that his laboratory research was extrapolated unfairly to enhance the Commission's central conclusion that there was a link between depictions of sexual violence in media and aggressive behavior toward women in real life. In rough summary, Donnerstein found that college-age men exposed to certain violent films (X-rated and R-rated "slasher" films) were statistically more likely to deliver simulated shocks to women subjects. He contended, "All that you can show in these studies is that they're affecting people's attitudes." I observed in the same article that "highly charged, twenty-year-old college students get excited and press buttons, but if you can regulate material on the basis of attitudinal change, then the First Amendment has no meaning."

As the Commission got even closer to issuing its report, *The Washington Post*'s Lloyd Grove took a close look into what the *Post* called a "descent into the world of porn" by the Commissioners. He began with sentiments expressed by psychiatrist Judith Becker, who said the only thing she wanted was a steaming shower after the Houston trip. "The hygiene in these places is upsetting, and the viewing rooms and booths just smell bad back there." Ms. Tilton concurred, "It was a rest-room ambiance—the floors were sticky, the air was musty. I was astonished at the ability of some people to be sexually aroused in a place like that." Grove asked for my response, "It reminded me very much of a day in sixth grade when someone brought a dead cat to school," a kind of fascination with the unexpectedly disgusting.

I was described in this lengthy piece as "the Commission's chief antagonist" whose presence was "one of the things that made being a Commissioner an often-thankless task" because of my "searing ridicule." Indeed, I was delighted to be an "irritant." Other irritants Grove wrote about were Dobson's claim that he was once $1,500 behind in receiving his travel reimbursements, and a caricature in publisher Al Goldstein's *Screw* magazine of several commissioners participating in a dubious activity with Edwin Meese. Dietz had been warned that his life might be threatened by participating but admitted, "There were no threats."

Alan Sears thought it amusing that taxpayers were paying for magazines like *Pregnant Lesbians* and *Tri-Sexual Lust*, noting that it was even hard to get clerks to give him receipts for what he had to characterize for reimbursement purposes as "educational books and literature." Several of the commissioners described to the reporter the dilemma of disposing of dildos given to them by sexologist Ted McIlvenna. They were left in a hotel room, lost, taken home but locked in a file drawer away from a child, thrown in the garbage. The article described me as finding some of the events excruciatingly boring, for example, a late-night session in Scottsdale listening to Dial-A-Porn tapes for nearly an hour. "If that's not dull, I don't know what is— sitting around in Arizona, wishing you were out in the desert air but instead listening to 57-second messages about anal intercourse."

At about this time, reporter Bob Scheer finally scored an interview with Commission Chairperson Hudson, then the federal prosecutor in Arlington County. We met immediately following that interview so I could drive him around Arlington County to see what Hudson's "clean up" campaign had achieved. Bob mentioned that one of the disturbing tidbits he learned was that Hudson had not read a book during the past year. Bob wanted to go to some bookstores and buy an adult magazine but couldn't find so much as an issue of *Playboy*. He insisted we go to the one and only "gentlemen's club" still operating in the county, where we found a few bored dancers (non-nude with a few pasties) roaming the place. Bob just kept repeating that he was shocked by what he didn't see.

I always enjoyed hanging out with Bob Scheer, including going with him one night to Elaine's, a New York restaurant where he introduced me to its owner Elaine with whom he had gone to high school. Our buddying culminated with a weekend stay at the Mayflower Hotel in

Washington where he asked Carole Vance and me to help fact-check his final article on the Commission for *Playboy*.

The Porn Commission's Final Report

Just a week before the official public release of the Final Report, it was sent to the commissioners. Since I won that legal challenge demanding all access to their work and it was Memorial Day weekend, I decided to try to disturb them one more time by releasing the report myself. The monstrosity was 1,960 pages in two volumes with deep blue covers. It contained ninety-two recommendations for policy changes. Knowing that no one would ever read something of this length, particularly on a three-day weekend, I summarized it in an accompanying press release, and I offered to duplicate it for the press. I made sure to include the appendix called "Examples of Materials from the Report of the Attorney General's Commission on Pornography." This appended document contained alphabetized lists of 2,345 magazines, a similar number of films, and 725 books that had been located during a commission staff visit to the still extant "Times Square dirty bookstores" and similar locations in five other cities. This listing amounted to what I called "a national bibliography of pornography, complete with graphic descriptions of every conceivable—and some inconceivable—sexual practices." How detailed was this report? There was a description of all sixty-three individual photos in *Tri-Sexual Lust*. The report included the full scene-by-scene descriptions, along with complete dialogue from several widely popular adult films of the time, including *The Devil in Miss Jones* and *Debbie Does Dallas*, along with more obscure classics like *Biker Slave Girls*. I concluded the press release with a personal observation that I found much of this material offensive but, "Just like Larry Flynt has the right to publish *Hustler*, the federal government has the right to publish its adult materials too."

FREE STREAM

HOSTED BY

e**X**otica
PRESENTS

TWO GIRLS
ONE MIC

FEATURING
MINISTER & FORMER EXECUTIVE
DIRECTOR OF AMERICANS
UNITED FOR SEPARATION OF
CHURCH & STATE
BARRY LYNN

THURSDAY | 2/11
6 PM ET

ALL EPISODES AVAILABLE ON
WWW.EXXXOTICA.TV

ALICE VAUGHN

YVETTE D'ENTREMONT

Ad for porn podcast that featured Barry Lynn on porn and civil liberties in the U.S., three decades after the Porn Commission.

When this little press release hit the offices of *Good Morning America,* a producer called, saying she wanted me to catch a flight to New York Monday night to be on Tuesday's show. She did note that, if I didn't want to interrupt my weekend, I shouldn't put out something so interesting on that weekend. Of course, the whole point of putting this out on a holiday weekend was to give reporters something they wouldn't have to work too hard on over their weekend while maximizing the publicity the ACLU would get. That segment was hosted by Joan Lunden, now best known as spokesperson for A Place for Mom, a senior care referral service. It featured a short debate between a representative of New York's Women Against Pornography (WAP) chapter and me. The WAP representative called pornography a "roadmap for rape" and I countered that it was mainly just an adjunct to masturbation. When the segment was over, I apologized to Lunden for using the word masturbation. She just laughed and said, "Oh, we'll get a lot of mail about that."

This truly was the last straw for Hudson. Although they couldn't bar me as a member of the public from lining up and watching their final press event at the Justice Department, I was relegated to an "overflow room" with a television streaming the events in the Great Hall of Justice next door. As reporters and twenty-seven television cameras were gathering, I noticed that many of the journalists were looking up after hooking their microphones in at the speaker's podium, then shaking their heads or giggling. As soon as the camera shifted to a wider shot, I could tell why. There was an enormous statue of the Greek goddess of justice with one exposed breast. Hudson would give the report to Attorney General Meese standing under a statue with a naked breast. The photo was on the front page of virtually every newspaper in the country the next day and graces the cover of this book. Although not necessarily proud of this, I often referred to it as "the three boobs" photograph in subsequent presentations. One journalist noted that Meese himself had reported that he had not had a chance to actually read the report, nor would he comment on the possible pornographic nature of the statue behind him.

The following day I happened to be walking past a statue outside the Library of Congress and saw a tourist family looking at the mermaid breasts on that statue and laughing, commenting that it was just like the photo in that morning's paper. At this point, I thought, "Maybe ridicule has worked." Indeed, James Dobson himself came up to me in a Washington restaurant about a year after the Commission had finished and said, "You know I hate everything you stand for, but I must admit, you destroyed all the good work we attempted to accomplish."

On report release day, I held my own press conference a few hours following theirs, and the pack of press that had watched the morning release virtually all showed up at mine as well. I made a brief statement that concluded, "Most of the Commissioners would be happy to tell all Americans not only what they can have in their libraries, but also tell them how they can behave in their bedrooms." I was asked what the whole yearlong investigation had proven. "All this proves is that if you give a biased, pro-censorship commission a half a million dollars and a year, they will write a lopsided pro-censorship report at the end."

I pointed out specifically that three of the four women members of the Commission dissented from some of the voluminous recommendations. This wasn't a big surprise to me. Dr. Becker and I had lunch a few weeks before the end of the Commission's work in New York and she said, "I have never seen one rapist where I could connect his violent acts to pornography viewing." She was nearly that blunt in her dissent, joined by Ms. Levine, "No self-respecting investigator would accept conclusions based on such a study, and, unfortunately, the document [we] produced reflects these inadequacies."

Other comments came in from supporters and critics, including this from Al Goldstein, publisher of *Screw*, a newspaper in New York City kept alive mainly by ads from massage parlors (non-therapeutic in any medical sense) and escort services: "What will they try to outlaw next, Dove Bars?" Goldstein's culinary interests may have helped lead him to his post-porn career: greeter in a bagel shop.

Hudson went on to be confirmed as a federal district court judge. Alan Sears became executive director of a right-wing law firm specializing in "family issues," after a brief stint as the associate solicitor for surface mining at the Interior Department. The *Newsletter on Intellectual Freedom* of the American Library Association, referring to his original job change, wrote, "Washington was swept by a round of predictable jokes about taking the strip out of strip mining," then noted that the Interior Department's recreational bookstore was selling *Penthouse* and *Hustler*.

In Lloyd Grove's article noted above, he asked some of the commissioners and staff if, given the concern that pornography is dangerous to public health, it may have had any adverse effect on them. Lezar responded, "Ask me in ten years," while Dobson acknowledged that he had thought about that but, "It didn't." For one of those associated with the process, though, the answer turned out somewhat differently.

Dobson and Father Ritter were the most traditionally "religious" members, often voicing their religious beliefs during business meetings. I was a little late to one afternoon session and found myself listening to a discussion, led by Ritter, of whether Michelangelo's statue of David could be considered pornographic. By a narrow vote, the Commission decided the answer was "no."

Shortly after that discussion, reports began to surface about Ritter's own sexual activities. He resigned from his post at Covenant House when officials discovered that he had at least one inappropriate relationship with a young man at the facility. Rumors had also surfaced that he might have been purchasing the company of young men (not children) to stay in his hotel room as he was attending a Commission hearing. This turned out to interest the New York City attorney general. Before the investigation began, the Franciscan order, of which Ritter was a member, urged him to seek counseling, which he refused to receive. He moved to India to finish his ministry, and then lived in seclusion in a small town in upstate New York until his death from cancer in 1999. His saga is sadly a pattern followed in many "abusive priest" cases.

For several years, during the tenure of the Commission and in the years following its report, I was a popular speaker about it. I even addressed the Adult Video Convention in Las Vegas in 1986. Paul Fishbein, the editor of the group's magazine, stated his approval of the 188-page ACLU report called, "Polluting the Censorship Debate," particularly enjoying my statistics about home video. I pointed out that only 28% of homes had a VCR and that 9% admitted to renting X-rated videos, which might indicate that, by the time every home had one, 32% of Americans would be renting porn, "This is a not an insubstantial level of interest in this material." The group published a monthly magazine called *Adult Video News* which had a boatload of sexually provocative but non-nude photographs advertising new adult films. As I was flying to Nevada, I looked through the most recent copy and noticed that there were a disproportionately high number of actresses with the last name "Lynn"—and I could imagine many viewers of television news seeing stories about the Commission with me being interviewed and then seeing the marquee of an adult movie theater with the name of an actress surnamed "Lynn" on it. Did they wonder if we were related?

At the convention, I addressed this directly, "I was looking at your magazine on the way out here and just wanted to say definitely that neither Amber Lynn nor Ginger Lynn are related to me." I then paused and showed them one page of the magazine, with a blonde woman leaning over the hood of a gold colored sportscar, noting "But

I am still checking on Porsche Lynn." John Weston, the very capable attorney that the group used, was in general a person not given to joking around, and I was never sure he appreciated my commentaries when we shared a platform. However, he did give a marvelous retort in a Supreme Court hearing when asked, following his repeated references to the First Amendment, whether he didn't think that America's fighting men would assume that the First Amendment was designed to preserve great works of art. He said he thought they would "be more likely to be fighting for *Playboy*."

The trip to Las Vegas was paid for by one of the two largest distributors of gay pornography in the country, Steven Toushin, who was straight and had a conventionally attractive woman with him when we had dinner the night before my speech. This was the only time I was actually eager to get invited to some industry party, but that didn't happen. I went back to my room at Caesar's Palace to sleep in the round bed in the room with a mirror on the ceiling, and, across the room, a hot tub.

Performers as Always are Center of Attention
Continued from page 26

Ginger Lynn -- looking as good as ever

Ginger Lynn at the Adult Video Association conference in Las Vegas where Barry Lynn detailed the operations of the Meese Commission to gales of laughter, including saying, "Ginger Lynn is not my sister."

My host in Las Vegas was later convicted on federal pornography charges and spent several years in prison. I only learned in 2020 that the other major purveyor of gay pornography was a San Francisco straight Jewish couple, Karen and Barry Mason, whose story was chronicled in a Netflix documentary called *Circus of Books*. The store they ran in North Hollywood was one of the few safe places the community could buy things and meet in those days before internet shopping and dating. The Masons were threatened with imprisonment but avoided it by destroying their entire inventory and closing the shop under a plea agreement.

During my one and only appearance on the *Oprah Winfrey Show*, I was on with an anti-porn Christian lawyer and was scheduled to arrive on set immediately following two child molesters live from a Utah state prison. Technical difficulties emerged and a producer ran frantically into the Green Room and said we had to be on set immediately. In these last moments, I thought the lawyer probably had heard I had been at that Vegas convention, so I joked, "Yes, they put me up in a fancy hotel with a round bed and a mirror. When I woke up in the middle of the night lying on my back and looked up at what I saw, I started to think you guys might be on to something." He actually responded seriously, saying that "We'd be glad if you came over to our side." His total lack of a sense of humor became one more reason to find him annoying.

Following the Meese Commission report, Don Wildmon and I appeared in many debates, most notably on *Meet the Press*. Incidentally, this one appearance got me invited to the 25th Anniversary Dinner for *Meet the Press* held at Union Station in Washington. As it happened, this was the same night as one of my appearances on *Crossfire* with Jerry Falwell, where I observed to a crowded live audience that, rather than have politicians hang up the Ten Commandments, it would be better if more of them just observed them. *Meet the Press* was broadcast a week or so after the Meese report and featured *Playboy*'s Christie Hefner, Hugh Hefner's daughter, and Henry Hudson for its first half and Wildmon and me as the second half. Wildmon acknowledged that he hadn't even read the Report and rejected panelist Eleanor Randolph's claim that if he re-published the Report, which he had considered but never got around to doing, he would be mass-producing pornography because of the extremely graphic descriptions of the material in it.

Barry and Christie Hefner of Playboy speak at an ACLU event.

I criticized his call for vigilante action against stores that carried even *Playboy* and *Penthouse.* He said they were breeding grounds for looking at even worse material and then engaging in criminal activity. I supported his right to picket but stated, "Is it right to use those powers toward the end of regulating what other people can see and read? To get a book out of the library? To get a film off of the video dealer's shelves? I think it's just as wrong to do that as it would be for atheists to get together and try to drive a Christian bookstore out of a shopping center. Constitutionally protected? Yes. Wise. No." The end of the show devolved into one more mind-numbing effort to conflate child pornography with every other kind of sexually explicit material.

Wildmon and I also had a question-and-answer session in *Video Review* magazine. I was asked whether the facts that so many stores were carrying X-rated tapes and that consumers were spending upwards of eight million dollars yearly constituted a "serious social problem"? My response, "What it represents is that people are interested in seeing sexual materials on video...not a social problem but a widespread social phenomenon." The amount spent on explicit materials was always mentioned. As John Weston, the adult industry's most frequently employed litigator, often pointed out, this was unlikely to represent eight people buying a billion dollars' worth of porn each. I also warned in this interview that if you give censors an inch, they will drive much farther: "Censors are never satisfied—it is like feeding raw meat to a dog. They come back. Censors will keep coming back to the video store until there is nothing left but *Pinocchio* and *Snow White*." I said this with some irony, because virtually every fairy tale had already been turned into a porn parody.

Wildmon's most utilized tactic throughout his career was the boycott. *Playboy* asked me to do a few short articles on Wildmon's boycott tactics after much of the Meese Commission dust had died down. These articles described the successes of his boycotts, which turned out to be somewhere between slim and none if the measure of their success was an assessment of how many people took the steps the organizers wanted and whether the boycotts directly affected corporate policy or profits. When Dr. Martin Luther King, Jr. took on racial segregation in Montgomery, Alabama buses, or Cesar Chavez urged refusal to purchase specific kinds of produce, they did undoubtedly stop bad practices: buses became integrated and worker conditions improved when economic pressures were brought to bear.

But Wildmon's claim of success requires a little closer analysis. Books and magazines are central to public discourse. Moreover, they are clearly different from lettuce leaves, which cannot even be read by fortune tellers.

In his heyday, Wildmon claimed to have succeeded in stopping corporate practices he and his followers disapproved of by getting masses of people to refuse to shop at those companies. I found that, when items were removed, it was never because of the number of complainants Wildmon brought out. It was sometimes due to a fear of what might happen. One specific example of Wildmon's exaggerating the boycotts' impact concerned the hotel chain Days Inn, which used a satellite television provider named Hi-Net to provide adult films. Wildmon urged that his members call the reservation number to object. When I did that and talked to the national night supervisor, he said he had only three calls about the movie service, characterized as, "one moral complaint, your call and a call from a guy in California who wanted to sell us a movie."

The Feminist Critique

Running in tandem with the Meese Commission was a serious effort to deal with pornography not so much as a criminal matter, but as a civil rights concern. In 1984, the Indianapolis City Council had passed an ordinance which defined the use, display, or commercial transfer of many forms of sexually explicit material as forms of "sex discrimination." This strategy had been crafted mainly by law professor Catharine MacKinnon and activist Andrea Dworkin. The American Booksellers Association sued the Mayor and in 1985, convinced a unanimous Seventh Circuit Court of Appeals that the ordinance was unconstitutional on its face. This approach created controversy within the feminist community and MacKinnon and Dworkin tried to revive interest in it during their testimony before the Meese Commission.

Our first discussion of this was a private conversation in my office late one afternoon. Frankly, it was one of the most serious conversations I ever had about this topic—it was the epitome of what one cannot see or hear anywhere in the media: deep and personal discourse about the meaning of pornography, the effects it may have on men and women, and why the civil rights approach was or was not any different from traditional efforts to use the criminal law to regulate it.

The Commission had difficulty dealing with the feminist approach to pornography. It listened to MacKinnon and Dworkin and other women critics of the material with more respect accorded to them than to members of, say, the Feminist Anti-Censorship Taskforce (FACT) but seemed to have trouble fully comprehending what remedies were being sought.

As a person who considers himself a feminist and whom many feminist activists consider an ally, I took these critiques by feminists seriously. I had many debates about this specific approach, one with a DC-based activist, Martha "Marty" Langelan. I am including my opening statement here as an example of the somewhat differently nuanced approach I took when not discussing this with a religious zealot or politician.

I'd like to tell a story about a pig. Some months ago, in a town near Cincinnati, Ohio, a group of citizens sought to have the children's book Charlotte's Web—*about a talking pig—removed from library shelves. Why? The citizens said that God had not created talking animals, and any suggestion to the contrary, e.g., talking swine, was blasphemous. They did not consider themselves censors. They simply knew they were right. Ms. Langelan resists the use of that word to describe herself as well. I cannot concede the moral high ground to any censor. Whether the subject is a children's book about a talking pig or a "men's magazine" with a pig's eye view of women, it is always wrong to use the power of the state to suppress that which you find offensive or which you feel leads to "harmful attitudes."*

Ms. Langelan always speaks eloquently about a variety of harmful effects from the use of sexually explicit materials. Let me say right now that some of the specific injuries she mentions can be remedied through legal mechanisms which do not offend any constitutional guarantees of free expression in any significant fashion. For example, a woman sexually harassed by a co-worker who places centerfolds on her desk regularly to humiliate her can bring actions under Title VII of the Civil Rights Act and recover damages from those who cause or allow this harassment to occur. In most states, a woman coerced into sexual activity she did not want–even by her husband–has been raped or sexually assaulted, whether the idea came from her husband's fantasies, a porn film, a PG-rated movie, or the Oprah Winfrey Show. *Sexual assault is actionable. Some states already have causes of action for "invasion of privacy" that permit money damages and even injunctions when a picture is published in an unauthorized manner, as in the production of "coerced pornography." In other words, these harms are real and already have remedies. I do find it unfortunate that Women Against Pornography and similar groups expend so much energy trying to delude* people into thinking they are powerless just because there are no "Indianapolis style" ordinances on the books.

Some of the other things she discusses, though, are problems for which the law should provide no remedies, even though they are expressions of very hurtful ideas. I'll get to that shortly.

First, though, let me venture into the "meaning" of pornography. Obviously, Ms. Langelan has catalogued a plethora of the most violent and nauseating images one can find on the pornographic landscape. I've got to defend the right of even those images to exist. To put this in some perspective, though, it is important to realize that the few longitudinal studies on the nature of pornography (don't think about that phrase too much in this context) show only a small—and possibly declining—percentage of sexually explicit material to be of a violent nature. Most porn is simply words and pictures depicting consenting adults engaging in consensual sexual activity.

Moreover, the actual function of pornography is far more complex than what Ms. Langelan suggests and is thoroughly consistent with the purposes for which the First Amendment was created. It is very easy to forget, amid bestiality and genital mutilation, that we do not need a free speech and press guarantee to support ideas that are not threatening to anyone. We need it when it does shock, does offend, and does challenge persons' perceptions in a significant way.

Porn does have political significance, like so many other forms of speech. Looking at what Ms. Langelan and I would agree on is the negative side: It can communicate that women like to be or should be subservient to men. Regrettably that is the belief that has held sway in Eastern and Western cultures since the beginning of human history. It is, however, quintessentially political, concerning the distribution and use of power in social relationships. In fact, the unanimous panel of the Seventh Circuit Court of Appeals that held the Indianapolis ordinance unconstitutional rejected the claim that pornographic material had "low value" because the ordinance supporters "believe that this speech influences social relations and politics on a grand scale, that it controls attitudes at home and in the legislature."

The "subordinate women" view is not the only message of porn. It often also promotes a particular view of sexuality which does not include traditional values like responsibility, romance, and privacy. Put bluntly, it asserts that it is good and healthy for people to engage in sex with many people (preferably simultaneously) in many places in many positions. That doesn't happen to be consistent with my sense of morality or aesthetics, but my opinion and, frankly, anyone else's opinion, should be irrelevant to consideration of what others want to communicate in whatever way they choose to do so.

But there is more. The social message of some pornography is seen as beneficial to the authors' self-identity and self-understanding. Now that pornography has transcended its early, nearly exclusive focus on young women's breasts, there is a message that all people are "sexual beings." Contemporary sexually explicit publications include portrayals of pregnant women and 55-year-old grandmothers, as well as the increasing appearance of once-shunned images of male genitalia. This is not a negative development. Acknowledgement of sexual diversity helps everyone understand sexuality in a healthier manner. For sexual minorities, most of whom are not involved in any violent or abusive lifestyles, material that depicts and affirms those lifestyles can be a method to acquire real self-understanding. Self-awareness, like political statement, has been a fundamental purpose of the First Amendment.

Pornography also legitimatizes the exploration of fantasy, without any necessary relation to intended conduct. When the Feminist Anti-Censorship Taskforce filed a brief against the Indianapolis ordinance it noted, "Depictions of ways of living and acting that are radically different from our own can enlarge the range of human possibilities open to us and help us grasp the potentialities of human behavior, both good and bad. Rich fantasy imagery allows us to experience in imagination ways of being that we may not wish to experience in real life...."

Some suggest that porn works on your irrational impulses, not your intellect. True indeed, but the fact that porn asserts its worldview graphically and not analytically doesn't change its First Amendment status. Even the Supreme Court, in a case called Flast v. Cohen, *assessing the impact of a defendant in a draft resistance case having entered his trial court wearing a jacket emblazoned with words suggesting that people have sexual intercourse with the Selective Service System, upheld the right to put "Fuck The Draft" on your clothing, declaring, "We cannot sanction the view that the Constitution, while solicitous of the cognitive content of individual speech, has little or no regard for the emotive function which, radically speaking, may often be more important."*

Producers of communicative material should have the right to choose any mechanism or medium they choose. If individuals want to argue the merits of oral sex, they should not be accorded lesser constitutional protection if they preach it in a graphic porn film rather than in an article in the Journal of Sex Research. *And where would Dr. Ruth fit in?*

But Ms. Langelan and her colleagues point out that porn serves as a special and uniquely damaging way to contribute to gender inequality. This is also a claim I must reject. No reasonable person could suggest that the status of women is higher in rural Alabama where there is little porn than in Manhattan where there is lots of it. Was the status of women higher in 1930 in the days of pin-ups than in the 1980s where a glimpse of stocking (or pubic hair) is no longer shocking? Are women's lives better in Saudi Arabia without porn or in the United States where $8 billion dollars of the stuff is sold?

And there is little reason to believe that porn is anything close to central in the subordination of women. Porn is actually quite easy to avoid. You can walk down 99.8% of America's streets and never see a graphic, sexually explicit image. Any image related to subordination of women is far more likely to be generated by anything from the commonplace necklace ads that say "chain her in 14K gold," the ultimately helpless heroines in Harlequin romances, or the cartoon Smurf world run by little blue men with but one giggling Smurfette. Porn has no magical power that sets it aside from these other cultural images—not even its power to generate a male erection.

Is there a connection between porn and sexual assault? It is undeniable that there are examples of media portrayals of sex and/or violence whose elements are replicated almost identically by persons during the commission of a criminal act. These isolated occurrences do not permit broad intrusions into First Amendment rights. As I said to the Ed Meese Pornography Commission recently, "We can't suspend the First Amendment because an image or idea causes the most suggestible person who hears it or sees it to behave in an anti-social manner."

The "made for television" movie called The Burning Bed was the most widely viewed such film in the history of television. It prompted thousands of telephone calls from women to crisis centers seeking help in combating spouse abuse. However, one man did set his wife on fire, mirroring the action of the abused wife against her husband in the film. Under a First Amendment calculus heavily weighted toward restriction based on anecdotal evidence, this film would also be restricted. Vicious sex crimes have been well-documented to be "connected" to public stimuli as varied as the golden-calf scene in the Cecil B. DeMille version of The Ten Commandments or an Anglican church service.

Ironically, the more pathological an individual is, the less likely it will be that we can determine just what will set him off. Pedophiles when arrested often have in their home not only commercial child pornography but scrapbooks containing underwear advertisements from Sunday newspapers. If the measure of suppression was what some material caused a handful of people to do, we would all be reduced to sitting in silent, darkened rooms to prevent errant sounds or images from crossing the eye or mind of someone who would react in an antisocial manner.

Aren't there new "laboratory" studies that show the negative impact of pornography on college age males? All of them are subject to serious methodological criticism and *arguably substitute simple stimulus and response analysis for highly complex long-term patriarchal conditioning. But forget that. The research in some ways just proves the obvious. If you show men lots of porn in which women appear to "like" being raped, and then ask them in a questionnaire "do women sometimes enjoy being raped"—more will say "yes." That does not mean they become rapists any more than listening to the President on television discussing "Reaganomics" will turn you into a fiscal conservative. Some of the same social scientists who do these studies have also found that if you "de-brief" the subjects by explaining to them the fallacies of the "rape-myth," they become more sensitive than when they began the experiments. Chalk up another victory for the First Amendment—good speech drives away bad speech.*

If we drive out pornography under the premise that it causes "bad attitudes" about sex or the role of women, we will be embarking on one very slippery slope. I am not going to stand here and say, "If today, Hustler goes, tomorrow we lose the book of Leviticus." My problem is that if we allow the transfer of bad, really bad ideas and attitudes to suppress Hustler, we have substituted a kind of "intellectual mob rule" for the First Amendment.

Feminism is the greatest intellectual challenge of the 20th century. Its strength comes primarily because it has challenged and successfully challenged a variety of suppositions regarding male dominance and patriarchy. Feminism has challenged them by meeting them head-on and persuading people of the errors of previous ways of thinking about power balances in our culture using the eloquence of The Feminine Mystique and the organizing of Bella Abzug. I want this critique to continue. It is by the creation of positive, alternative images, not the governmentally assisted suppression of negative ones—that this progress will continue. If we give free rein in our culture to the notion that courts can tell us what is the "proper" kind of sex, or the "politically correct" relationship between men and women, it won't be long before we are slouching back to a sexual dark age.

The Feminist Critique of pornography is, in my view, although largely erroneous, still enormously important. My comments in the debate with Marty were my best effort to summarize the unique arguments from parts of this community.

Child Pornography

After most of the major television appearances I did on the subject, I would get letters from ACLU officials about what a fine job I had done and then a reference to "even with the impossible issue of child pornography." The ACLU's policy was that obscenity laws and child pornography laws were unconstitutional. I disagreed on the issue of child pornography and the Supreme Court had agreed with me in a unanimous 1982 decision, *New York v. Ferber.* The Court found that preventing sexual exploitation of minors was a compelling "government objective of surpassing importance" and upheld prosecution of those selling such materials. I argued that prosecuting persons who had made "kiddie porn" did not prevent the principal injury to the children. Much child porn was made by parents and other persons related to the victims. This closeness of the criminals to the victims made many prosecutors reluctant to get involved. But the idea that you couldn't prosecute persons who filmed the sexual abuse of children was ridiculous.

By February 1985, I went to my immediate supervisor Morton Halperin and said, "Mort, this policy is absurd and no one in the organization except me ends up going on television to defend it. It should be changed, but maybe I could write a policy that focuses on sexual privacy and remedies for its invasion that could start to reverse it." He agreed and I wrote a memorandum for consideration by the Board of Directors in its spring 1985 meeting. It was called "Pornography and Sexual Privacy" and made the case for changing the policy to permit prosecution (or at least civil remedies) when a person of any age was coerced or could not give meaningful consent to participation in filmed sexual activity.

I knew that many ACLU supporters were concerned that if the organization made a sweeping assumption that no minors could agree to be in pornography, it might run afoul of its strong commitment to allowing minors access to contraception and abortion without the need for parental consent. Although I thought it would be easy to draw a distinction, I also knew that taking this head-on would get us nowhere. Perhaps we could focus less on age and more on coercion of persons at any age.

As indicated above, I had numerous debates with feminist legal scholar Catharine MacKinnon and, although I thought she was considerably off base in many of her conclusions, she was completely accurate about certain matters involving direct coercion. She represented, for example, a woman named Linda Marchiano (better known as Linda Lovelace during her appearance in the film *Deep Throat*) who claimed that she had been physically coerced into making that movie. If a ten-year-old child can't give consent to being in a sexually explicit film and assuming the truth of Ms. Marchiano's statement (which I did), there should be a right to "sexual privacy" that civil libertarians would bless. The ACLU applauded reproductive privacy regarding abortion and contraception and sought its extension into the area of sexual behavior (including same-gender relationships). We approved of evidentiary rules that prohibited disclosing an individual's past convictions for prostitution, asking would-be employees about her or his sexual history, or using one-way mirrors or wiretaps to obtain information on marital infidelity.

The ACLU went further, however, and embraced certain civil remedies for "invasion of privacy" torts. ("A tort is an act or omission that gives rise to injury or harm to another and amounts to a civil wrong for which courts impose liability." *https://www.law.cornell. edu/wex/tort#:~:text=Definition,1.*) An invasion of privacy tort refers to the theft of a property right in the commercial value of an individual's personality or performance. The Supreme Court in 1977 held that there was no First Amendment protection of "free speech" when a man who made his living being shot out of a cannon at a carnival was filmed and his act shown in its entirety on the air by a news station. After his Supreme Court victory he apparently settled with the television station (common in such cases) but I can find no reports of what actually occurred. The ACLU approved of that decision and even supported a New York statute that created fines for the unauthorized use of one's "name, likeness, or persona in the commercial endorsement of a product or service with which they are otherwise associated." So, if our Executive Director at the time, Ira Glasser, had his face put on a billboard next to a loaf of raisin bread, and he either didn't like that kind of bread or didn't want to appear to endorse it, he could sue for compensation. Surely, I noted, there were analogies to be found here. The final point in my position paper was that what allegedly happened to Ms. Marchiano was a particularly horrendous form of sexual assault, a term which the ACLU preferred as a moniker rather than "rape" because it encompassed a wider range of forcible sexual acts.

And there should be remedies even if the technical "statute of limitations" had run its course, including criminal fines and forfeitures of proceeds directly attributable to the products resulting from the coerced act. Compensatory damages were awarded for emotional distress, for use of the stolen item, and even for recovery of lost earnings. For example, if a nude photograph was used in a "sleazy" publication, it would be unusable in a "higher class" magazine (yes, there was such a case in New York in 1981).

This analysis seemed "foolproof." I even noted that it would not necessarily make it illegal to film a minor who "chose" to be in a pornographic film. However, the debate on this matter at the Board meeting went on for several hours and the policy was not adopted, one Board member claiming in a passionately weird address that it would be seen as "giving in to pro-censorship feminists." It took the ACLU another twenty years to come up with a slightly more sensible position on child pornography; it has never adopted a policy on coerced production of adult pornography.

Porn after the Commission

Some of the post-Porn Commission events were memorable. Here are four.

First, I had a debate at George Washington University one Saturday night where I was joined on the anti-censorship side by *Hustler's* Larry Flynt. The pro-censorship voices were the host of the event, evangelist and radio host Bob Larson from Colorado and another Meese Commission observer named Michael McManus, who wrote for several religious magazines. The discussion was well attended and included a bizarre incident where Larson walked up to me, thrust a photograph from a porn magazine in my face and asked, "What do you see here?" I responded that it "appears to be a blonde woman engaging in oral sex with a black-haired man" but then added, "I must say I have never been forced to see such an image in my life by somebody opening it in front of me. Why'd you do that?" He did not respond. This being a college-age audience, attendees were disinclined to be on the Larson bandwagon. Larson kept doing radio shows and speeches about pornography until it lost its luster as a fundraising topic. He recently moved into the presumably more lucrative field of casting out demons.

The second curious event was at Princeton University in late November 1986, a two-day extravaganza featuring Larry Flynt giving a lecture and a panel discussion where I was joined by Alan Sears; actresses Seka and Gloria Leonard; a former police officer, Norma Jean Almodovar, who had recently become a prostitute; and law professor Catharine MacKinnon, who proposed pornography was a violation of civil rights.

I had done an interview for ABC's *20/20* shortly before this debate, concerning whether some of the so-called "feminist pornography" being produced by directors like Candida Royale could be declared "obscene" by juries anywhere in the country. The host, libertarian-inclined John Stossel, had his staff send me a few of Candida's videotapes, which I dutifully watched. One of them starred Gloria Leonard. They had been produced by Femme Productions, a genuinely woman-owned and operated video production company of what it called "feminist pornography" that made roughly seven films per year. I said on camera that the films would not be deemed obscene anywhere and it would be a waste of time for anyone to prosecute them as "obscenity."

Princeton housed all of us on campus and some of us joined the university's various "eating clubs" for dinner. On the way to the event after dinner at a student club, I was walking with Gloria, who commented that she had really enjoyed that recent appearance of mine on ABC's *20/20*. Gloria then asked, "But what did you think of the content [of my film]?" I wanted to be diplomatic, even though I didn't find them particularly compelling cinema, so I just said, "You are a fine actress but maybe they could have used better music."

To my knowledge, no recording of the Princeton event exists. At its conclusion, Catharine said, "We put on a good show for them," which was probably accurate. She had refused to have dinner with students; but she was, as usual, quite eloquent during the debate itself. There were occasional remarks about me being an apologist for the pornography industry. Andrea Dworkin regularly said I was a "shill" for the industry. I disagreed. The industry and I were not that close. Evidence of this was that at Princeton the porn actresses all left the auditorium before I even spoke.

The event was well covered in *The Newark Star Ledger* the next day with its reporter noting that, "Lynn of the ACLU was the sole panelist who was a member neither of the porn industry or some anti-porn cartel. And the audience, mostly graduate and undergraduate students, seemed to realize this, giving him its loudest applause of the evening as he countered points made in the slide shows." He quoted me, "Women will not cure sexism in our society, will not eliminate their earning of 59 cents for every dollar a man makes, by terminating Larry Flynt's right to be Larry Flynt." He also quoted Gloria, who had observed, "The First Amendment was not created to protect mom and pop and apple pie but to protect unpopular forms of expression. That's what pornography is."

Many years later when I was doing talk radio, my producer at the time, Dianne Robinson, arranged an interview with the very same police officer from the panel. Ms. Almodovar was still making the case that prostitution was more honorable than being a cop. As I led into the commercial to proceed my exchange with her, I said, "Next, I chat with a hooker I slept next to in New Jersey." When we went on air, I clarified that we had been in adjoining rooms at the Princeton guest house that night of the panel.

The third highlight was an all-day symposium at the august Smithsonian Institution in Washington called, Restraint of Speech in A Free Society: The Limits of the First Amendment. I always wondered who spent their entire day listening to a group of "experts" talking about anything, but I found the audience to be quite engaged as four law professors (including Fred Schauer, a member of the Commission), several writers, the co-authors of the Minneapolis "civil rights" ordinance against porn, Catharine MacKinnon and Andrea Dworkin, a director of the Hirshhorn Museum, and I chattered away for over seven hours. That conventional debate closed with a more unusual last section on "The Arts." By this hour, I was getting tired and frankly a little bored when someone asked all of us to "define art." I'm not proud of myself about this, but I said, "My definition of art is any image painted on black velvet that includes images of unicorns, Elvis, or the Last Supper." That was pretty much the closing comment of the day.

In those days I also spoke at academic and journalist debates. Once, my debate partner was Franklyn Haiman, a well-respected communications professor at Northwestern University, who began his presentation with a spirited defense of the often-censored novel *Lady Chatterley's Lover*. This seemed almost quaint, as his lead-off opponent was Commission member Park Dietz, who displayed a seemingly endless set of slides involving genital mutilation. Porn had changed, but Haiman didn't seem well-prepared for those developments. My belief was that if you wanted to take a "no censorship of pornography involving adults" position, you had to be willing to embrace the right of the most repulsive material to exist.

Legislating on Porn

I suspected for almost the entire year of its existence that whatever the Commission came up with would provide the basis for new legislation to be considered by Congress right before the 1990 elections. This was the subject of my trip to Vegas. Thus came the introduction of something called The Child Protection and Obscenity Enforcement Act.

I testified in both the House and Senate Judiciary Committees against many of the provisions in the bills that became this act. Perhaps the strangest moment was an exchange with Arizona Democratic Senator Dennis DeConcini about the large number of rapists who claimed they were imitating scenes in pornography as they committed their crimes. I pointed out to him that "there are a limited number of acts in which one can engage in the sexual arena. And for someone to say, 'Well I engaged in anal sex, and I had looked at a picture of it' doesn't tell us enough to form a conclusion that, except for the pornography viewing, that rapist would have become a Sunday School teacher. It also does not explain why such an enormous number of people admit to seeing pornography yet do not become criminals."

As it came down to the last few days of the 99th Congress, pieces of this legislation were attached to an omnibus anti-drug bill at the insistence of Florida Republican Congressman Bill McCollum. This thing could not be stopped, but I had thought it possible to eliminate some of its most "dangerous to free speech" provisions. My experience was that getting constituents to support the right of pornography to exist by writing a letter, much less making a telephone call was a tall order. After consulting with a few of the women at Femme Productions, I thought of a new approach: why not have famous adult film actresses call the owners of the hundreds of small "mom and pop" video stores to get those owners to call their members of Congress asking them to oppose any provision that violated the First Amendment? Such late-in-the-session calls only needed to come into the House Judiciary Committee to have any effect: most of Congress was already in full campaign for re-election mode and everybody on Capitol Hill wanted to get out of Washington. There would be two days at most of negotiations among staff members to get the final bill into shape. I did what I could to work with the staff, but I knew there would be limits to what I could accomplish. The little tactic did work, as a number of actresses including Seka (one of the most famous and financially profitable folks working) made those telephone calls. A staff member for Congressman Bob Kastenmeier (D/WI) called to report that, "Members are getting a lot of calls from porn stars, and I suspect you have something to do with that."

I was pleasantly surprised at the number of provisions that were removed from the bill. These included making it a crime to possess for personal use any "obscene" material in a public park, building, or military base; making it a new federal crime to order "obscene" material over the telephone, even if the order was placed by a person who had not seen that material and thus knew nothing of its contents. Also removed were several extremely broad forfeiture provisions that a store's owner would lose all of her or his inventory if they rented even one "obscene" video; and provision for a civil fine of up to $500,000 for a person selling any item declared "obscene" anywhere in the country, thus nationalizing the community standard from the *Miller* case.

Plenty of bad ideas did get incorporated, though, including making it a federal crime to "possess with intent to distribute" any obscene item (instead of criminalizing only using the mails to send such matter), broad new wiretap authority, and the requirement that anyone producing actual—but not simulated (another major victory)—depictions of sexual activity (including "lewd exhibition of the genitals") prove that the person was of legal age and keep records of where consumers and law enforcement persons could find that proof on file.

The record keeping provision was prompted primarily by the story of Traci Lords (given name, Norma Kuzma, the subject of a multi-episode podcast released during the COVID-19 pandemic). She was found to have made approximately seventy-five explicit films when she was under the age of eighteen. California authorities searched her home and found false identification. In that state at the time, there was a defense of "reasonable belief" when it came to engaging in some unlawful conduct with minors. One detective told *The Los Angeles Times* that "in appearance, she does appear to be older than she really is." Federal prosecutors took over the case in August 1986, but they emphasized that Ms. Lords herself was not facing charges.

Many video store owners were concerned because Ms. Lord's tapes were popular and had generated considerable income. Some local prosecutors stated they would move aggressively to prosecute store owners who had profited from this "child pornography," which this technically was. Government officials were seeking assistance, sometimes in return for lighter treatment, from industry persons about the industry's knowledge of Ms. Lord's age. Some did cooperate and claimed that the adult industry didn't take age verification seriously, but Ginger Lynn (remember, not my sister) told me decades later that she refused to cooperate even though she was facing tax evasion charges and had to spend a few years in prison.

At roughly the same time, the 6,000 members of the National District Attorneys' Association approved a policy to "vigorously" enforce obscenity laws, based on the organization's sense that Ed Meese had elevated this enforcement to a higher level. A U.S. Attorney from Utah claimed, "I would expect that, within the next twelve months, there would literally be an explosion of cases on the federal level."

However, to my surprise, that explosion never happened. A brief flurry of activity occurred in the early Nineties with a high-profile case chronicled in *Entertainment Weekly.* The film company Cal Vista and two of its officers were indicted on multiple counts after undercover FBI agents posing as video store owners ordered a few X-rated videos at a Las Vegas convention and had them shipped to Broken Arrow, Oklahoma. These indictments for interstate transportation of obscenity had taken close to a year to bring. Attorney General Dick Thornburgh claimed that it "stakes our commitment to aggressively pursue large-scale producers of illegal hard-core pornography...in every state of the union." I told the magazine that this was a classic sting operation and a perversion of law enforcement. There wasn't a problem in the community, but the Justice Department spent resources going after them anyway. Frequently the defendant will agree to a fine or to get out of the business completely to avoid court costs and the risk of losing. The case involving the film *Sorority Pink*, which starred, among other people, Porsche Lynn (again, not a relative) ended up a year later in a mistrial because the jury couldn't agree that it was obscene.

In the first twenty years of the new century, one can locate few cases in the entire country. Child pornography prosecutions occur, but obscenity arrests are rare and convictions even rarer. In part this is because jurors like those in Oklahoma, who are part of the community that needs to determine if their standards have been violated, are often unwilling to convict. Perhaps because they have seen similar material themselves, they know that seeing it does not require trips to adult bookstores to buy or rent videos or adult theaters to see them on a big screen.

A flurry of interest did occur in the mid-Eighties in using the Racketeer Influenced and Corrupt Organizations (RICO) Act to prosecute purveyors of obscene materials, something included under RICO only in 1984. The purpose of this statute was to have a better tool for going after organized crime. The first successful prosecution of this kind came against two Northern Virginia videotape sellers named Dennis and Barbara Pryba who had been alleged to have distributed $105.30 worth of videotapes in interstate commerce. A blockbuster article by Arthur S. Hayes in *The American Lawyer*, however, found that three women on the jury, who voted to convict, had serious reservations about what they were doing. One of the women said, "I thought to myself, 'These people sell dildos to adults. They were going to take away someone's house for that?'"

These jurors also noted that they were not aware at the time they voted for conviction that their decision could lead to prison sentences of up to ninety-five years, fines of $785,000, forfeiture of their businesses (valued at one million dollars), and even personal property like their home (worth $1,900,000). The jurors were also surprised to learn post-conviction that the judge in the case disallowed defense evidence that the same videos being used in this prosecution were for sale at other rental stores in Virginia and that polling showed high tolerance for the sale of sexually explicit material. In the article, my friend, attorney Bruce Ennis, predicted the case would go to the Supreme Court. It was indeed appealed but review was not granted, although a strong minority of members wanted to take it and specifically noted they wanted the case reversed. RICO prosecutions fell out of favor for obscenity as the years went on, but Henry Hudson (remember him?) who prosecuted the Pryba's case continued to support its use. This was a perfect example of where a jury could have used, had they understood it, the doctrine of "jury nullification" to determine that the statute was inappropriate.

The most publicized obscenity trial in the past fifteen years involved Rob Black (a.k.a. Robert Zicari) and his wife. The case was covered in PBS and BBC documentaries (I am in the latter but haven't seen it). Black's prosecution stemmed from a postal inspector near Pittsburgh, Pennsylvania, ordering five videos and downloading six video clips from the internet in 2003. Black's company was in North Hollywood, California, and the Pittsburgh area prosecutor, Mary Beth Buchanan, undoubtedly thought it would be easier to get a conviction in more conservative western Pennsylvania than in Black's "home territory." These titles were the worst she could find in his sales division, *Forced Entry* (three rape scenes), *Extreme Teen 24* (an adult woman dressed like a young girl is convinced to have sex by an older man), and *Cocktails 2* (consumption of many forms of bodily fluids). She also agreed that little had been done following the Meese Commission activities, "Lack of enforcement of federal obscenity laws during the 1990s has led to a proliferation of obscenity...such as the vile and disgusting material charged in this case."

Initially, Black (Zicari)'s attorney convinced the trial judge to drop all charges, arguing that since "possession of obscene material" was not a crime, there should be a privacy right to obtain that material as well. When the Justice Department appealed that decision successfully, Black and his wife gave up for lack of funds and were sentenced to one year and one day in federal prisons.

Some years later, during my time with Americans United for Separation of Church and State (AU), I had many run-ins with Commissioner James Dobson. However, before I moved to AU, he was embroiled in one more censorship and pornography issue: several hours before Ted Bundy's Florida execution, Dobson obtained an interview with Bundy, notorious serial killer and rapist implicated in at least thirty-six violent crimes, who told Dobson that he became a murderer because he was influenced by watching R-rated "slasher" films, reading detective magazines, and coming across a bundle of *Playboy* magazines someone had thrown out in a park he walked in as a teenager. Bundy ominously announced, "There are forces loose in this country, particularly against this kind of violent pornography where, on the one hand, well-meaning decent people will condemn the behavior of a Ted Bundy while they are walking past a magazine rack full of the very kinds of things that send young kids down the road to be Ted Bundys."

INQUIRY

Topic: CRIME & PORN

The Rev. Donald Wildmon, 51, has been a United Methodist minister for 32 years. Wildmon is the founder of the American Family Association, which is headquartered in Tupelo, Miss. He is the author of several books, including The Case Against Pornography. *He was interviewed by USA TODAY's Barbara Reynolds.*

Donald Wildmon

Bundy told truth about pornography

USA TODAY: In his last interview before his execution, mass murderer Ted Bundy said his life had been warped by pornography and sexual violence in magazines, movies and TV. Were you surprised he said that?

WILDMON: That's not shocking to me at all. I've got letters from people in prison who killed people and from people who have been victimized, and they all say the same thing.

USA TODAY: Do you have any examples?

WILDMON: I have a quote from Arthur Gary Bishop, who was executed in Utah in 1985 for killing five young boys. He called himself a "homosexual pedophile." The boys he killed were usually from age 4 to 10. Bishop, in his confession, said pornography was the thing that motivated him. He said the same thing that Ted Bundy said. It's nothing new. I've got a letter that we're going to use in ... next magazine. It come in last week from a man in

We can't believe what Bundy said

Barry W. Lynn, 40, legislative counsel for the American Civil Liberties Union, sees danger in trying to stop violent crime by censoring pornography.

"There just is no credible scientific evidence that links acts of violence to pornography," he says.

Convicted serial murderer Ted Bundy claimed, in a pre-death interview with Dr. James Dobson, that pornography fueled his violent acts.

But, says Lynn, "I would no more rely on Bundy's psychological self-analysis than I would rely on his stock market advice. This man has built an entire life out of lying to people and getting away with it."

Lynn believes that even if Bundy was propelled to violence by pornography, ideas and actions shouldn't be regulated on how the most suggestible people will respond.

Barry Lynn

"If we did that, we'd end up sitting in caves, watching black television screens and looking at wordless newspapers," Lynn says.

The Constitution guarantees us the right to see sexually orientated materials, says Lynn, unless they fall within the narrow definition of obscenity.

"People may say, 'What value does this have?' That's not a question that the Constitution generally permits us to ask. We don't have to justify every newspaper article or every television program by some aesthetic or moral standard," he says.

Most people who have seen pornography don't become criminals, says Lynn. Some will find it erotic, some will find it disgusting and the majority will find it unappealing.

— Barbara Reynolds and Sonya Ramsey

Don Wildmon and Barry Lynn discus serial killer Ted Bundy's claim that "pornography made me do it."

Dobson ate all of this up as proof positive that all kinds of sexually explicit and violent non-explicit material was leading directly to murder. Dobson was all over the media pointing this out. The *TODAY* Show had a debate two days following Bundy's execution on January 24, 1989, between Gene Abel, a psychiatrist and medical director of the Emory University School of Medicine's Behavioral Medicine Institute and none other than Park Dietz. Abel responded to the host's question about the credibility of the comments of a "mass murderer" by noting he took them "with skepticism" and that he found no correlation in his clinical practice between the use of pornography and criminal behavior or aggression.

Dietz disagreed and indicated that about half of sexual sadists like Bundy had sizable collections of pornography when arrested; "It fuels their fantasies, gives them new ideas, and makes this look like a more normal activity since millions of people expose themselves to it." Both physicians agreed that a troubled home life and alcohol were major components of sex crimes. Dietz opined that curbing pornography would be better in making society safer than banning assault rifles, to which Abel responded, "The sadist can carry around the deviant fantasies in his head. He doesn't need pornography to get such a fantasy." Similar debates occurred for weeks thereafter. Dobson's final interview with Bundy was sold on video for a $25 "donation" to his ministry.

Ted Bundy's crimes came to the attention of many Americans because of a book by crime writer Ann Rule. She had actually been a college student with Bundy and had a breakout volume called *The Killer Beside Me* about their relationship. Having often interviewed Ann on the radio, I called her when this story of Dobson's first broke. What did she think? It took about a nanosecond for her to say, "Barry, this is Ted Bundy's final scam." She frequently repeated that answer in public presentations over the next few weeks.

Regarding the Bundy-Dobson tape, I told *USA TODAY* that I would no more trust Bundy's psychological analysis of himself than I would trust him to give advice on the stock market, "This man built his entire life lying and getting away with it. Even if this was his one true statement, we can't regulate based on how the most suggestable person reacts If we did that, we'd end up sitting in caves, watching blank television screens and looking at wordless magazines."

I didn't see much of the people I shared television studios and debate platforms with after the great legislative maneuvers of the 1990s. In 2008, Nadine Strossen, longtime President of the ACLU Board, decided to resign and a major luncheon celebration occurred in Washington at the ACLU's Biennial Conference. I was asked to participate in the tribute to Nadine and was paired with Christie Hefner. We worked out a routine that was a bit more engaging than some of the other pairs of tributers. As soon as we began, I said, "I am always a little intimidated when I am next to Christie Hefner. I am afraid that she will look at whatever I am wearing and take me to the side of the room at the end of the event and say, 'Barry, don't you ever read the fashion articles in *Playboy*?' Then I will be the very first man in the history of the world to say 'No I never read any of the articles. I only bought it for the pictures.'" A local right-wing newspaper quoted that observation the next day.

I learned a great deal about human sexual conduct spending time with the Commission. Indeed, I came to believe that virtually all of the "conservative" opposition to it was based on a repulsion to the conduct being depicted. For the Right, it was bad enough that gay people could not be arrested for "sodomy" in their own homes, and it looked like marital unions and perhaps same sex marriage were shortly coming down the road. It was unthinkable that such conduct could be depicted visually where children might see it and "turn" gay.

For anti-pornography feminists, I think the opposition is more nuanced and unfortunately not well understood. Although the Commission heard from Catharine MacKinnon, Andrea Dworkin, and representatives of Women Against Pornography, there was only one recommendation even dimly related to those testimonies: an urging that legislatures "hold hearings and consider legislation" to provide for some civil remedies for persons harmed by pornography. The 7th Circuit had already declared one such ordinance unconstitutional. To this day, I think civil libertarians ought to embrace ideas of sexual privacy that not only permit access to pornography but work to create real remedies for persons who are coerced into appearing in it.

Finally, I think it would be good for more people to be honest about their reactions to graphic material. Nina Totenberg of National Public Radio once asked me what I personally thought of porn. I said, "Some of it is truly disgusting, but I will admit that some of it actually turned me on." In the aforementioned Lloyd Grove article, he asked the same question to which I responded, "I don't think any male Commissioner could honestly say that none of this was erotic, that none of it was sexually appealing. Certainly, some of it was to me. The failure [of the Commission] to ever acknowledge that was an oddity I found very strange." When I would say these things, there would usually be one colleague on the ACLU staff who would say, "Why do you even admit this?" My response was, "If a reporter asks the right question, I will give her an honest answer."

Porn in Phones, Computers, Mail, and the Arts

Following the Report of the Meese Commission, Congress repeatedly tried to weigh in on specific media that it thought contained offensive or dangerous sexual content. One of the fiercest battles was over so-called Dial-a-Porn which was a multi-billion-dollar business in which people could call a 976 exchange or a 900-telephone number and hear taped salacious messages or have conversations with actors and actresses. Since these numbers could be reached by anyone calling those exchanges (even if it was a toll call) the concern was that minors would access this programming. Senator Jesse Helms (R/NC) and Congressman Tom Bliley (R/VA) took the lead in trying to stop dial-a-porn.

There had been some highly publicized cases of young people who became so enamored of making calls to these services that their parents turned their children's obsessions into *cause celebres*. In one instance, a father made the rounds of major television shows discussing how his son committed suicide after his calls were stopped by parental disapproval. I appeared with him on *Good Morning America* and made the same arguments I made before Congress about how federal prohibition of these messages would intrude on the right of adults to listen to these messages if they chose, and that this highly private means of communication did not require any third-party involvement like booksellers or film theaters would. I suggested some constitutional means for restricting access by minors using call blocking, access codes or other technologically available alternatives.

When our segment was over, the father and I and host Charlie Gibson were standing off to the side and I asked the father what his response had been when he discovered his son was making these calls and whether that response might have been so harsh that his son had reacted to it by killing himself. He was shocked to be asked and immediately rejected any complicity in his son's decision. I was not persuaded.

Senator Helms and Congressman Bliley introduced legislation to amend the Communications Act to completely prohibit the "knowing" transmission of "obscene" or "indecent" material over the telephone. This language was designed to replace the extant language that only prohibited such transmissions to minors and allowed an affirmative defense to prosecution if service providers and telephone companies took specific steps to curtail access by those minors.

On December 2, 1987, the Senate passed this bill as an amendment to a big education authorization package, a solution I thought was unconstitutional on its face. Mort Halperin and I communicated with the House leadership about how bad this approach was and offered some alternative language. The House voted in February of 1988 to "accept the Helms amendment," but in a second vote defeated Helms' language 200-179 and instructed conferees to deal with this issue. Indeed, I had specifically sent the House conferees proposed language that would handle the whole issue by developing regulatory fixes and technological solutions instead of criminal sanctions.

My proposal was to require any common carrier that provided listening access by multiple callers to a live or recorded voice message or chats be available only through telephones whose subscribers specifically requested this kind of access or from telephones after the caller entered the number of a credit card. This seemed sensible: "dial-an-anything" (from porn to a chat with Santa Claus) only through subscriptions or use of private "calling cards" issued by the telephone company. This had numerous advantages, including being subject matter neutral. After all, did parents worry solely about the sexual content or also about the enormous bills their children were running up by calling numbers advertised on cartoon shows to get daily updates on their favorite characters? Some had argued that wily children could steal the "calling cards" from their parents, but this would amount to a negligible number of children. The ACLU sent a formal letter of support for this Conference Committee language, but the compromise we offered was ultimately rejected.

I had personally reached out to Congressman Bliley with whom I had worked to stop bans on tobacco advertising (described below) to show him that the First Amendment works best if it is seamless and protects everyone's preferred communications. After one meeting between just the two of us, Bliley said he would try to sell this technological fix to the anti-pornography advocates who had convinced him to get involved in this issue to begin with. About a week later he called to say they had rejected the idea and were insisting that the complete phone sex ban move forward. He acknowledged that this was what he had to do, conceding to the press when the hardline ban was approved by the House that, "in an election year, voting in a style (perceived as) weak on pornography is not a very good position." I was irate that the Religious Right advocates couldn't see the value of my technological fix and condemned the passage of the bill as a "hopelessly inept effort to deal with the issue of children's access to dial-a-porn."

The ban resulted in two things, one silly and one judicial. By the start of 1989, the Federal Communications Commission had staff members listening to pornographic telephone messages to try to figure out which were "obscene" or "indecent." The FCC's enforcement head, Gregory Vogt, said obscene ones involved words describing "kinky sex" and "offensive sounds." Multiple courts and ultimately the entire membership of the Supreme Court in *Sable Communications v. FCC* in 1989 found that the coverage of "indecent" programming in the prohibited category was unconstitutional. Three Supreme Court members also found the coverage of "obscene" messages also unconstitutional. In 1993, however, the same dial-a-porn company went to the Supreme Court to have declared unconstitutional restrictions on obscene telephone communications, but, in a brief and unexplained order, the Court rejected considering that issue.

In the mid-Eighties, the advent of personal computers changed everything. Many of us at the ACLU were convinced to use Kaypro computers where the screen and keyboard were conveniently self-enclosed in a green metal case. At this stage of computerization, the main law enforcement issue was electronic bulletin boards where one could find obscene material, child pornography, or advertising for the availability of child victims, which Henry Hudson absurdly claimed "are uniformly homosexual in nature." The Reagan Administration supported efforts of Virginia Republican Senator Paul Trible to pass his Computer Pornography and Child Exploitation Prevention Act in 1985. Naturally, as always, an effort emerged to merge child pornography and adult sexual materials. It prohibited the interstate transportation of "obscene, lewd, lascivious or filthy writing, description, picture, or other matter entered, stored, or transmitted by or in a computer" and penalized anyone who "knowingly owns, offers, provides, or operates any computer program or service having reasonable cause to believe" it is used to transmit such material.

As usual, I testified for the ACLU when Virginia Republican Senator Paul Trible's bill came up for a Senate hearing in the fall of 1985. I suggested that even if one accepted the idea that "obscenity" could be an exception to the First Amendment under some circumstances, regulation of graphic sexual material observed or produced in the privacy of one's home was not justifiable. Such a standard was equivalent to "prosecuting a letter carrier with a federal crime for delivering *Hustler* magazine, because some courts have considered some issues of it obscene."

By this time the ACLU had changed its child pornography policy just a bit and had concurred with me in part that the production of visual depictions of sexually explicit conduct was a violation of the rights of children when these acts cause substantial physical harm or continuing emotional or psychological harm to those children. The ACLU still had the position that once this horrific stuff was produced, its distribution could not be criminalized. I argued that pedophiles kept lists and other information about their victims in computer files. These files were often the only evidence to prove the crimes had been committed.

The language of this Trible proposal was broad and vague, particularly in its prohibition of statements which "facilitate, encourage, offer or solicit sexually explicit conduct...with a minor, or the visual depiction of such conduct." I surmised, as did another witness who was in an Apple computer users' group, that this could ensnare teenagers who were running dating services, since dating did occasionally lead to sexual activity and the service could be prosecuted for "encouraging" or at least "facilitating" sexual acts with underage persons. I concluded that the bill would be unlikely to make any real contribution to stopping child exploitation and its "primary effect would be to saddle new computer technology with the moralistic regulation of older methods of communication."

In the fall of 1989, Senator Strom Thurmond (R/SC) also decided that something had to be done about the expansion of sexually oriented advertisements being sent through the mail. The law at the time allowed persons who didn't like what they saw in the mail to prevent future mailings of advertising that they found "erotically arousing or sexually provocative," by putting their names on a list at the post office to avoid receipt of any "sexually oriented advertising."

In testifying against Thurmond's approach, I summarized current law as permitting offended individuals to take individual trips to the trash can. I called Thurmond's approach "replacing individual trips to that trash can with a governmental presumption that all 'sexually oriented' ads belong there." I pointed out that the definition of "sexually oriented" seemed to be much broader than what was "obscene" or even "indecent" under federal law; it would cover "catalogues of lingerie and underwear, material that discusses AIDS or birth control and suggests purchase of condoms, and standard solicitations for lawful books, videos or other merchandise of a sexual nature." If the protection of children was the justification for new laws, I found it strange that Congress required sexually oriented material to be in an envelope marked as "sexually oriented." This seemed an open invitation to curious children to open it, being forewarned that it contains "good stuff."

This legislation never passed. In 1987, the Supreme Court in *Jacobsen v. United States* had dismissed the conviction of a Nebraska farmer named Keith Jacobsen who had been prosecuted in 1987 for possession of child pornography. His name and address had been found on a mailing list at an adult bookstore in another state. When he was arrested at his home, the only illegal item found was a magazine he had purchased after a 26-month campaign of government officials sending him catalogues from five dummy corporations offering child pornography and sending him surveys about his sexual interests. Five members of the Court held that "when the government's quest for convictions leads to the apprehension of an otherwise law-abiding citizen who, if left to his own devices, would never have run afoul of the law, the courts should intervene." The surveys were at most "indicative of certain personal inclinations" and a "person's inclinations and fantasies are his own and beyond the reach of government." Tragically, at least two defendants caught up in the same sting operation as Jacobsen committed suicide.

One of those justices overturning the Jacobsen conviction was Clarence Thomas. During his confirmation hearing, Thomas had been credibly accused by witness Anita Hill of engaging in sexual harassment of her when she was his employee. She told the Judiciary Committee that Thomas used crude sexual references around her and mentioned certain actions in pornographic films. Journalists were curious about what films he may have rented, but the owner of the video store at which the rentals were made properly refused to testify or present rental records, something I found to be a principled position to protect Thomas' privacy rights. When Thomas ruled as he did in Jacobsen's case, I said, tongue-in-cheek, that "maybe he was nervous his name was on one of those mailing lists."

The other most significant sexually oriented controversy during my ACLU years involved funding for the National Endowment for the Arts (NEA) whose funding had come under fire by the Religious Right for funding "blasphemous" art that combined sexual imagery with anti-religious bias. The first culprit was a display by Andres Serrano of a wood and plastic crucifix hanging upside down in a bowl of his urine. Notwithstanding his explanation that this was a representation of where Christianity had moved in recent years, its critics said that it compared Christ to excrement. Serrano had obtained a $15,000 NEA grant to produce this and other work.

The second major controversy was a grant to help fund the transfer and display of photographs by renowned photographer Robert Mapplethorpe to Washington's prestigious Corcoran Gallery. The Gallery received $30,000 to move this display from Philadelphia and show it in DC. After criticism of the photos for their "homoerotic" nature and a few photos involving sadomasochism, the Gallery cancelled the show. An uproar occurred about the cancellation and one evening some of the photos were projected by a local arts organization on the wall of the Corcoran. Shortly thereafter another gallery displayed the exhibition, which was seen by an estimated 40,000 people.

In light of these controversies, the director of a New York City gallery called Artists Space, which had received a $10,000 NEA grant for an exhibition to illustrate the effect of AIDS on the artistic community, reached out to the new NEA director, John Frohnmayer, and warned him of possible protests. The exhibit was called "Witnesses: Against Our Vanishing." Frohnmayer initially told the group to give the money back; but, after a meeting with its leadership, he courageously decided to process the grant.

Senator Jesse Helms in late July 1989 persuaded the Senate to cut the NEA budget by $400,000 and to prohibit the use of NEA funds for obscene or indecent materials or materials which "denigrate the objects or beliefs of adherents of a particular religion or non-religion." This action was taken by a voice vote. The House authorized a $45,000 cut and maintained the prohibition on funding "obscene" art.

I had sent to the conferees from the House and Senate, who would work out a compromise, a memo about the unconstitutionality of all this, particularly if it contained any language about denigrating religion. In it I pointed out that the Supreme Court had in 1952 struck down a licensing requirement that permitted the censorship of "sacrilegious" films and that a number of subsequent court decisions built on that *Burstyn v. Wilson* ruling, finding that prohibiting flag burning, vulgar rock lyrics, and "virulent ethnic and religious epithets" is unconstitutional.

All this controversy led to the termination in 1988 of all NEA grants to individual artists. Ten years later, the Supreme Court upheld the statute that authorized the NEA to take into account "general standards of decency and respect for the diverse beliefs and values of the American public." Essentially this was an instruction to self-censor.

It's Only Rock 'N' Roll to Me

When "Tipper" Gore, the wife of Senator Al Gore, was in an airport and heard part of a song by Prince called "Darling Nikki" that contained in the opening verse, "I met her in a hotel lobby/ Masturbating with a magazine," Tipper was unhappy. Along with a number of other prominent wives of Washington bigshots like Susan Baker, spouse of Reagan's Treasury Secretary James Baker, and the wives of Senator Bob Packwood and Congressman Tom Downey, Jr., Tipper decided to form a group called the Parents' Music Resource Center (PMRC). Although the group persistently claimed it was not in favor of censorship (no one ever is) their view of much popular music was, to say the least, hostile. Ms. Baker, for example, condemned Madonna for teaching young women "how to act like a porn queen in heat" and Michael Jackson for writing a song she said was about "sadomasochism." Other members referred to the songs of Sheena Easton, Twisted Sister, W.A.S.P. (the group persistently said it stood for 'We're All Sex Perverts'), and Cyndi Lauper as "negative" and "harmful trash" because, according to PMRC, they promoted rebellion, drug abuse, sexual promiscuity, perversion, violence, and the occult.

PMRC quickly got meetings with the chair of the Federal Communications Commission (FCC) and the head of the National Association of Broadcasters (NAB). The FCC indicated it would look into the matter and the NAB warned the 806 operating radio and television stations to examine the contents of rock music carefully. The group also wrote the head of the Recording Industry Association of America (RIAA) to demand that it create a warning label system for recordings, suggesting that X could be used for profanity or sexually explicit content; D/A for drug and alcohol use; and, of course, O for occult references. Also included were demands that offensive album covers be wrapped in opaque coverings and that record companies reconsider contracts with individuals and bands that produce music containing these ideas.

These powerfully connected women were not satisfied when the RIAA decided to place "advisory labels" on recordings with "offensive" lyrics. They sought more publicity, encouraging the seventeen members of the Senate Subcommittee on Communications to hold an oversight hearing on the crisis of rock music. Five of the Senators on the subcommittee had wives who were PMRC members. I wrote a letter to Committee Chairman John Danforth (R/MO) arguing that this hearing should not even occur because "the decision to hold hearings about song lyrics sends the unmistakable signal to writers, producers, distributors and broadcasters of this form of music that their actions are under scrutiny and that official intervention in the form of federal legislation could descend on them from the wings... The writers of these lyrics [you've invited to testify] should not even be expected to explain or justify their work in an official forum such as a Congressional hearing." I told Danforth I knew he was determined to hold the hearing but asked that my letter be included in the official proceedings–which it was.

Notwithstanding that letter, I was as eager as hundreds of other music fans to get into the hearing to watch whatever happened. I waited in line for several hours to get a seat. Right behind me was rock critic and spouse of one of Bruce Springsteen's managers, Dave Marsh, whom I had met before. As we were chatting, he mentioned that he was writing a book on 100 ways to fight censorship. When he casually mentioned that he'd like to "shut up" the PMRC, I reminded him that, if he wanted to force people he disagreed with to be quiet, he was kind of being a censor. He took my criticism well, included this incident in his final version of the book, and asked me to join panels on censorship when he saw me in the audience at places like Folk Alliance International conventions.

There was enormous press coverage of this hearing, but my favorite summary was written by the clever journalist Alex Heard for *The New Republic*. Heard ended his piece by discussing Senator Paul Trible's opening statement that this "may well be the most important hearing conducted by the Commerce Committee this year." A few minutes later Trible left.

The musicians who appeared were Dee Snider of Twisted Sister, Frank Zappa, who was originally part of the Mothers of Invention, and folk/pop singer songwriter John Denver. The PMRC was allowed to present a twenty-minute "worst of rock lyrics" presentation that finished with lurid lyrics from an unknown metal band called Dementor. They included references to "golden showers" and "anal vapors."

As you may know from my earlier book, I really liked John Denver and his music. Why was *he* testifying? He told the committee that his song "Rocky Mountain High" had been attacked for being pro-drug. Senator Gore interrupted his comments, suggesting that some "songs do seem to glorify suicide." Denver responded, "If I could only count the number of times that a child has come up to me saying, 'If I don't get your autograph, my mother is going to kill me....'" The audience laughed. Dee Snider told the Senators, "As a parent and a rock fan, I know that when I see an album cover with a severed goat's head in the middle of a pentagram between a woman's legs—

that's not the kind of album I want my three-year-old son listening to." The audience laughed again, more humor at this hearing than at any other I witnessed or participated in.

Two months after the hearing, at a press conference in November 1985, the PMRC, along with the national PTA and the RIAA and NAB, announced that they had reached an agreement on how to proceed. Record companies had two options if the music was "explicit" (never actually defined at the event): put a warning label on the album that reads "Explicit Lyrics- Parental Advisory" or print the actual lyrics to the songs on the back cover. For cassettes that don't have spacious covers they could simply note "See LP for Lyrics." When a journalist asked me to comment, I said: "This agreement is a defeat for free expression and the broadest possible artistic expression in this medium. I am afraid that record stores will not stock labeled records and that broadcasters, whose licenses are renewed by the federal government, will be wary of playing these recordings." Activist and record producer/manager Danny Goldberg, who had started a group called the Musical Majority, gave a mixed reaction and urged record companies to only use the "print the lyrics" approach, observing that it would gain the "good will of the community." I liked Goldberg but often thought he was hopelessly naïve. Just what community approval would be gained by printed lyrics by Mentors, "Listen, you little slut, do as you are told/ Come with daddy for me to pour the gold/Golden shower,,,all through my excrements you shall roam?"

More low points were to come in the anti-rock and rap movement in the late 1980s. The first was a revised policy of the Federal Communications Commission in April 1987 that increased actions against radio stations that broadcast "indecent" material. Under the new standard, "indecent" programming was defined as "language or material that depicts or describes, in terms patently offensive as measured by contemporary community standards...sexual or excretory activities or organs." Indecent material could be lawfully aired after 10 p.m. because children would not be likely to hear it, the FCC rationalized and unanimously voted to order a crackdown.

The FCC was concerned about both what Commissioner James Quello called "garbage" rock music and the proliferation of "shock jocks" who tried, generally unsuccessfully, to follow in the footsteps of

Howard Stern. At the time, the general counsel of the FCC was Diane Killory, who had alleged that Stern had "on a number of instances broadcast indecent material." The previous standard had proscribed only seven "dirty words" all uttered by comedian George Carlin in one of his routines. FCC's Killory conceded that prosecution of Carlin would be too difficult. She refused to be specific on the *TODAY Show* about what Stern had said that she found so offensive but that could not be prosecuted. I felt it was up to me to explain, so I did.

Stern and his co-host Robin Quivers had been discussing the gender of a puppet named Lambchop used by Shari Lewis. Stern had observed that since Ms. Lewis was able to put her hand all the way up inside the puppet it must be a girl, implying that if it was a boy her hand would run into a penis. The interview was conducted by Katie Couric in New York, while Diane and I were sitting next to each other in Washington. One of the camera operators with us thought the Stern explanation was so funny that, for a minute, I thought he was going to knock over his camera. Diane seemed embarrassed that this incident had been brought up.

This reminded me of one of my favorite cartoons published in Paul Krassner's *The Realist*. In it, a person giving an interview said he "didn't give a damn" but, since the word "damn" had been "bleeped out" by a television censor, the viewers, sitting and watching with "conversation bubbles" over their heads, were filling in the censored "damn" with stronger words like "shit" and "fuck."

I can only speculate that NBC lawyers watching thought my repetition of the Stern conclusion about Lambchop might put the network in trouble under the new standard for prosecution. I told *Variety* that it was doubtful that this policy would lead to many fines: "Who in their right mind thinks the FCC has the time to bring hundreds of enforcement actions?" I did claim that it would have a chilling effect on broadcasters. They might want to steer clear of offending the FCC and broadcasters might self-censor, avoiding "speaking out on sexual topics or airing music with sexual references." *Variety's* Dennis Wharton concluded his article on this with the somewhat ominous line: "For broadcasters, the decision marks a new era. The FCC, it seems, has just pulled the plug on raunch radio." Of course, the Parents Musical Research Center applauded this. In fact the FCC decision had little effect and the advent of satellite radio, which was not regulated by the FCC, essentially eliminated any lingering concerns.

In 1987 several high-profile rock and rap groups were actually criminally prosecuted under the new FCC ruling. Jello Biafra of the band The Dead Kennedys and several of his colleagues were charged with violating a California law prohibiting "distribution of harmful material to minors." The material was a poster included in their most recent album *Frankenchrist* that was a reproduction of a painting *Landscape XX* by H.R. Giger, an artist best known for his set design on the film *Alien*. Biafra and his co-defendants refused to accept a plea bargain. They maintained that, "With an eye to avoiding the wrath of moral vigilantes, many other distributors, retailers, and record companies themselves are imposing in house censorship. Laws are only one way for homogenizing a culture. Intimidation is another."

Although the PMRC had always claimed it was against censorship, it objected to the sticker being on the shrink wrap, instead of the album cover. They opposed the warning that the package contained a work of art that some people might find "shocking, repulsive or offensive. Life can sometimes be that way." To PMRC officials, this comment did not constitute "consumer information."

I met Jello Biafra in 1989 at a rally in Lafayette Park across from the White House when I was working on rap and rock censorship. He was joined there by Vernon Reid of Living Colour and the three singers who constituted the band Run DMC. I had a dental appointment in the morning before the noon rally and I was "feeling no pain" from heavy sedation when I got up to speak. I did a little review of censorship of music in America, saying, "Ever since somebody figured out that the thrill on 'Blueberry Hill' was not just looking at the stars, there's been an effort to censor what's said in rock music." I also mentioned that radical feminist Emma Goldman had said she didn't want to be a part of any revolution where you couldn't dance. I concluded, "I think the framers of our Constitution would not have wanted to create a constitutional revolution where you couldn't rap and you couldn't roll." My comments went over well. The guys from Run DMC came over to me to say I "had rocked the joint," which my children said was high praise. A rock music publication analyzing the whole event said, "this show belonged to, not an artist, interestingly enough, but Barry

Lynn of the ACLU. Lynn reflected on the history of anti-rock efforts, and in doing so gave one of the most rousing speeches of the day."

Comments on music censorship from Lynn, PMRC leader Susan Baker, and Jello Biafra of the Dead Kennedys.

Biafra contacted the ACLU in Washington where I worked to see if I'd give them a statement, which I was happy to do. This was my statement, "The poster in question, like Dead Kennedys music and visual art in general, lampoons the conformism of American society. That is preeminently political speech. We know it works because it annoyed the authorities enough to try to intimidate their critics into submission by calling them obscene. This persecution is a sorry example of just the kind of government abuse the First Amendment was designed to prevent." The Dead Kennedys included my statement in their next album. Prosecution of the band ended in a hung jury.

In 1990, anti-pornography crusader Jack Thompson successfully sued the group 2 Live Crew for obscenity in Broward County Florida. Thompson told the local newspaper this resolution of the suit was "great news. Children will no longer be mentally molested." He bemoaned that this was only a civil action, not a criminal conviction and urged that authorities bring criminal racketeering charges against the group and any stores that sold the album, As *Nasty As They Wanna Be.* The judge, Jose Gonzales in a sixty-two-page ruling wrote that the album "appeals to dirty thoughts and the loins, not to the intellect and the mind."

I responded to this decision and the arguments made by Judge Gonzalez by noting that the First Amendment not only applies to well-crafted intellectual discourse but also to "music, art and literature that is on the cutting edge." I pointed out that the finding of a judge in Alabama that the group's previous album was "obscene" had just been overturned and that I couldn't believe that any jury, even in the South, would find either album in violation of "community standards." The principal lawyer for 2 Live Crew, Bruce Rogow, successfully appealed the judge's decision to the Eleventh Circuit Court of Appeals, where it was overturned in 1992.

Although most of the censorship of music issues involved sexual material, 1989 also brought an attack on the song "Fuck Tha Police" by the group N.W.A. (Niggaz Wit Attitudes). This song was on the group's double platinum album *Straight Outta Compton.* The song was criticized in an official letter to Priority Records from the FBI's Milt Ahlerich, who claimed it "encourages violence against and disrespect for the law enforcement officer." Ahlerich linked it to the seventy-eight law enforcement officers who had been killed the previous year, asserting that the song was "both discouraging and degrading to these brave, dedicated officers." This letter had been released at that "anti-music-censorship" rally in Lafayette Park. Dave Marsh and I met with Thomas Boyd, a Justice Department official, to discuss the FBI official's letter. Boyd told the press the meeting was "useful" but declined to accept our claim that the letter was attempted censorship. I had explained that under racketeering laws it was quite conceivable that the entire contents of a record store could be seized if a single item declared "obscene" was found, under the theory that the proceeds from that one item had been plowed back into the operation of the store.

As I and others had feared, the so-called "voluntary labeling" of records led to a flood of state legislation that built on the RIAA's support for labels. Some state bills specified that the labels be more specific and be affixed to records; others expanded existing laws to allow for civil lawsuits by parents if their minor children were sold "obscene" records. In Oklahoma, statutes were proposed that would prohibit attendance by minors at concerts where indecent lyrics might be sung. The Motion Picture Association of America had long battled governmental efforts to use their "voluntary" ratings system as part of state or local laws and were always successful. The same thing happened here. Virtually all such state efforts were blocked before they were adopted.

Cable Television: Stop Censorship and Enhance Public Access

Among the other issues I worked on at the ACLU, I fought efforts to restrain speech and worked to make the means of communication more accessible to the public. In 1985, Senators Helms (R/NC), Thurmond (R/SC), and Denton (R/AL) were trying to find a way to regulate sexually oriented programming on cable television. I had a protracted discussion with Senator Denton at the Subcommittee on Criminal Law of the Senate Judiciary Committee on July 31, 1985, in which I argued that "indecent" programming on cable could not be regulated because subscribers are able to not subscribe or to terminate subscriptions on cable that offended them because of sexual content or, for that matter, political or religious content. This consumer power made cable much more of a "private" choice than broadcast television and could not be regulated in the same way.

Before this hearing, several state laws that attempted to restrict the sexual content on cable had been declared unconstitutional;

those laws had used the same language as was currently proposed in Congress. They imposed significant fines and imprisonment for the dissemination of "any obscene, indecent or profane material by means of radio or television, including cable television." This was the only effort to include cable in such legislation. Although some cable services were running late night programming that contained nudity, that programming did not include actual sexual activity or even male nudity. I was only aware of a single cable system, in Bethlehem, Pennsylvania, where I grew up, that allowed a person to rent more explicit material that may have been declared "obscene" in other jurisdictions. The cable television industry had a bit more clout and cash than the dial-a-porn businesses or even record industries, and the bill banning indecent programming on cable never passed.

In the early days of cable television, the ACLU urged that cable be regulated like broadcasting since it was a scarce commodity, not a system of infinite abundance. The ACLU hoped that there would be a strong mandate for including both leased and public access channels. That didn't happen.

In the summer of 1987, I was asked by the National Federation of Local Cable Programmers to do an after-lunch speech at their national convention. This was not an issue I had worked on in much detail, but it was great fun to do a quick study of it.

I knew that the two state efforts to regulate "indecent" programming in Florida and Utah had been overturned by federal courts, and that the Utah case had been appealed to the Supreme Court, which had declined to hear it earlier that year. Not even four members of the Court wanted to examine the reasoning of the lower court decision. I also knew that the Cable Act prohibited owners from prescreening the programs on "access" channels. The law also prohibited cable station owners from refusing to air programs that they deemed too controversial.

I emphasized that some operators hated access channels and tried to make a false analogy with newspapers. According to one law review article, "Constitutional historians and laypersons alike would be alarmed if the United States government seized five pages of *The New York Times* in an attempt to increase public access to the media." This effort to be clever fell apart quickly, "When was the last time," I asked the crowd, "that you noticed the *Times* going to the City Council demanding that only the *Times* could be displayed in newspaper boxes and hawked in front of the Lincoln Tunnel?" In theory anyone can start a new newspaper, but cable would literally not exist except for governmental grants of right of ways to lay coaxial cable, string wires on utility poles, and put amplifiers under the street. Almost all community governments at the time (and many local governments still today) gave one cable provider a *de facto* monopoly and essentially protected that status by not permitting other companies into the market.

In the Washington metropolitan area at the time, there were three alternative "pay television" services: two scrambled over-the-air signals and one using microwave transmission. Two had already gone bankrupt and the third was on life support.

When Congress passed the original cable bill in 1984, its supporters issued a report that included, "A requirement of reasonable, third-party access to cable systems will mean a wide diversity of information sources for the public, the fundamental goal of the First Amendment—without the need to regulate the content of programming provided over cable." To me, these content neutral access rules were too modest an intrusion into the "rights" of cable operators as to be dignified by the characterization of an "intrusion."

Some litigation occurred. Cable operators tried to convince courts that both "leased" access (where a company pays to be on a cable system) and "public access" (where citizens utilize cable facilities to produce and promote special programming) violated their First Amendment rights. A frontal assault on public access had been rejected by a federal court in *Berkshire Cablevision of Rhode Island v. Burke*. In New York City some subscribers to Manhattan Cable insisted that the company was unwilling to deal with providers of unaffiliated programmers and asked for more pay movie services than HBO and Cinemax, which Manhattan Cable already provided. Manhattan fought this but in the temporary ruling, Judge Robert Sweet noted, "Despite the intrusion on an operator's discretion...a nondiscriminatory injunction to open up the wires of Manhattan Cable Television to non-affiliated programmers would 'neither favor one group over another' nor regulate the content of the speech...The Supreme Court has repeatedly admonished that the interest of viewers should be considered paramount in the First Amendment calculus."

In my speech to the National Federation of Local Cable Programmers I emphasized that the cable act and court decisions upholding access rights were not enough to make the promise of cable real. Community groups also needed cable companies to foster a multitude of programming and start promoting the access channels as "video soapboxes," informing their viewers where the "park" is and giving a boost to those who could use some help being lifted onto the soapbox.

This presentation went over well. The head of the association wrote me a follow-up letter about how "fabulous" it was and that the attendee surveys gave it "rave reviews." Although I deeply appreciated this feedback, I was even happier when a teenager and her mother came up to the podium and the young woman called it "life changing" and said she was now thinking of devoting her career to protecting free speech. Shades of Ramsey Clark, who had so powerfully affected the younger me, I thought.

Wiccans

Every child probably has something that frightens them on Halloween: ghosts, vampires, or mummies. For me, it was witches, or more specifically, Cackler the Witch, whose cut-out mask was on the back of a cereal box. She was ugly with green skin and a pointed nose and (presumably) an unpleasant cackling voice. Her visage and that cackle showed up in my nightmares as well. Little did I know that witches—Wiccans and pagans, male and female—would come to play a positive role in my life.

I did not know much about contemporary Wiccans until September of 1985 when, on the way out of the ACLU office to see my dentist, I got a call from a staff member for Republican Senator Bob Packwood of Oregon. She informed me that Senator Jesse Helms had just put some language in the appropriations bill funding the

Internal Revenue Service that forbade the IRS from using any money to grant or maintain a tax exemption for any group "which has as its primary purpose the promotion of witchcraft." Helms' language defined witchcraft as the "purported use of power derived from evil spirits, sorcery, or supernatural powers with malicious intent." "Should my boss [Senator Packwood] have objected to that?" Politely, I responded: "Yes indeed he should have."

I immediately called the United Press International wire service (at the time a genuine competitor to the Associated Press) and told them what had just happened, observing that the ACLU believed it "outrageous" (we were outraged a lot) that the government would give better or worse treatment to any group based on their religious beliefs.

I made it to the dentist and home just before Hurricane Gloria hit the Washington, DC, area with enough rain to close many roads by the next morning. I didn't get to work until one in the afternoon. When I arrived, I was handed fifty-some "WHILE YOU WERE OUT" notes, all from area codes and people, none of whom I knew. The callers turned out to be Wiccans and they were very unhappy with what Helms had done. They wanted to know what they could do about it.

For the next six weeks, America's pagan community organized to defeat the Helms proposal. I worked with them to get spokespersons on national television shows, prepare letters to the editor, and write to Congresspersons. By the time the House of Representatives' tax committee took up the bill, its members had been sufficiently educated that they literally laughed the language out of the bill. Thank the goddesses we did not have to set up a federal commission to determine what spirits were evil and which were good. That House vote occurred just one day before Halloween, giving the nightly newscasts a wonderful hook for a story.

I met so many fine people during this effort that I formed a longstanding commitment to the Wiccan community. When the head of President Bush's ill-conceived Faith-Based Initiative, Jim Towey, rejected the idea that "pagan faith-based groups" would be eligible for government funding, he noted, "I haven't run into a pagan faith-based group yet, much less a pagan group that cares for the poor...Helping the poor is tough work and only those with loving hearts seem drawn to it." Towey had been a lawyer for Mother Teresa and this arrogant statement was disposed of by pagan supporters who pointed out that they had the same heart as he did and that Pagan Pride groups alone had contributed 74,000 pounds of food and $51,000 worth of donations to homeless shelters recently. Chicago pagans had helped fund a battered women's shelter, and Massachusetts pagans had given thousands of dollars to help children with AIDS.

This prejudice against the Wiccans erupted many other times, as if the bigots had been infected by Hansel and Gretel tales or perhaps never got over their fear of those Cackler masks. Wiccan Cynthia Simpson was told by a federal appeals court that the Chesterfield, Virginia, Board of Supervisors could bar her from getting in the rotation to perform a prayer before its meetings. Board members called the Wiccan faith "a mockery" and said Ms. Simpson couldn't do the invocation even if she "was a good witch like Glenda" from *The Wizard of Oz*. In Titusville, Florida, when the City Council unanimously agreed to start its meetings with prayer and agreed to the request from a group of Wiccans to participate in giving the invocations, a cadre of over fifty Christians showed up to recite the Lord's Prayer in a successful effort to drown out the Wiccan message.

Courts were *sometimes* more open-minded and constitutionally sober when it came to pagan rights. When an Indiana family law judge granted a divorce decree requiring that the son of the divorcing couple not be exposed to any "nonmainstream religion," knowing that the son's father was Wiccan, the appeals court overruled his decision.

Perhaps the most important lawsuit in modern Wiccan history was the Pentacle Quest. The year was 2006. And I had moved to a new job, executive director of Americans United for the Separation of Church and State (AU). Former Georgia Congressman Bob Barr (R) was outraged when he heard that pagans were holding worship services on military bases. With ridiculous stereotyping, he said "What's next? Will armored divisions be forced to travel with sacrificial animals for Satanic rituals?" Barr's opinion, it turned out, was shared by President George W. Bush, who tried to stop the Veterans' Administration (VA) from adding the sacred symbol of a pentacle (a five-pointed star in a circle) to the list of emblems of honor that servicemembers' families could ask to be placed on their loved ones' headstones in VA cemeteries. The VA granted 38 emblems to a vast number of American religious groups, and even to atheists and humanists, but there would be no emblem for pagans. Widow Roberta Stewart of Nevada, whose husband had been killed when his helicopter was shot down on September 25, 2005, while flying a mission in Afghanistan, requested a pentacle for his headstone. Sgt. Patrick Stewart was on his second tour in the Middle East and was a decorated pilot. But VA officials acting on the wishes of the Commander-in-Chief denied the symbol of Wiccans.

July 4, 2006, ceremony at Arlington Cemetery where Wiccan priestess Selena Fox and Barry Lynn memorialized first headstone that included both a Christian cross and a Wiccan pentacle. Source: Circle Sanctuary.

I had the honor of meeting Roberta at a pagans' rights rally in Washington and hosting her and the senior minister of her church, the Rev. Selena Fox of Circle Sanctuary, at a little picnic at our house. The next day they met with AU legal staff and agreed to have us represent them in a legal challenge to the VA's withholding the Pentacle as a grave marker emblem for Ms. Stewart and a number of widows from the Korean and Vietnam wars. The case was filed and the Bush Administration and Attorney General, Alberto Gonzalez acted like they would fight us vigorously. Eventually American United's Legal Director, Richard Katskee, got a phone call from the Department of Justice that they no longer felt they could defend not granting the emblem. In April, 2007, we announced the settlement of the matter at a press conference in Washington. Roberta and Selena did media interviews at our AU office. As Selena was about to do an interview with National Public Radio, one of the attorneys brought her a copy of the official Veterans' Administration regulation form that had the day before depicted each of the thirty-eight emblems of honor. That morning it had been modified to include the new Pentacle emblem. Selena looked at it for a long time and I would swear that a light flowed out of her body. This is the only time this Christian witnessed what we might call "transfiguration."

The Wiccan community continued its efforts to get other pagan symbols adopted There are now sixty-five VA-approved symbols.

We continued to work on problems Wiccans had with government bureaucrats, including an Arlington, Virginia, court clerk who would not allow a priestess to conduct a wedding because the regular venue for the rituals of the group she represented was not in a physical building but outdoors. That only took a day to resolve.

Frankly, I had never expected to have my photograph on the front page of the *Stars and Stripes* newspaper, a publication that reports daily on military news. However, on July 4, 2008, Selena Fox and I celebrated at Arlington National Cemetery the completion of the first headstone acknowledging the burial of a couple, one Christian and one Wiccan, including their respective symbols. Several prominent Wiccans, including National Public Radio correspondent Margot Adler, who had written a book titled *Drawing Down the Moon,* took part in that incredibly moving experience. Reporters observed the ceremony, including a photographer for *Stars and Stripes*, whose picture of us appeared the next day.

Many pagans are in the military, including those who worship the Norse God Thor. A few years after the Pentacle Quest was completed, a pastor in California announced he was praying imprecatory prayers for my death. When that hit the newspapers, I received an email that a group of Thor supporters in the military were praying that a shield of protection be placed over me to cancel out the Christian death prayer. So far, it has obviously worked.

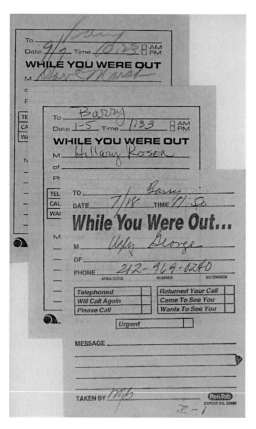

Before Voicemail and eMail, people left messages for call-backs on these pink slips. Here are a sample of hundreds concerning censorship that Barry Lynn received.

Chapter 2

EVERYBODY WANTS GOVERNMENT TO BAN SOMETHING

If you don't like photographs or videos of people naked or engaging in sexual activity, you might be inclined to want the government to censor it. As the Meese Commission discovered, however, there are differences in pornographic "products" and some people would just like to censor only some of them—the ones depicting violence; those involving "unnatural" (as in "statistically uncommon") behaviors; or only those depicting penetration but not nudity.

When you get outside of the porn realm, plenty of people would like the government to regulate, or even ban, other printed material. The ACLU opposed censorship of anything about any topic, and was concerned about any government efforts to limit the availability of material or impose penalties on people who produce, distribute, or exhibit unfavored material. The ACLU was not interested in governments supporting *some* speech or visual depictions over others. Governments must have no favored forms of speech or disfavored ones. For the years I was with the organization, I was involved in efforts to delay or derail a large array of federal efforts to restrict speech by favoring some examples over others.

Alcohol

Congress consistently tries to regulate speech about products that many members don't like, including condoms, alcohol, and tobacco. Solid constitutional law requires treating "advertising" of products, as "commercial speech," which has a presumption of protection under the First Amendment. The ACLU properly expected me to push hard to keep governmental hands off the regulation of this material.

In 1996, when for the first-time ads for alcoholic beverages appeared on television, a Washington-based organization called the Center for Science in the Public Interest (CSPI) took the lead in seeking increased regulation of alcohol advertising. Although beer was advertised on television frequently, hard liquor was never advertised; indeed television stations eschewed depictions of anyone even imbibing what appeared to be whiskey, tequila, or any of the other dozens of liquors on the market. CSPI and a coalition called Stop Advertising Alcohol on Radio and Television wanted to have Congress or the Federal Trade Commission craft a total ban on all alcoholic advertising on radio and television.

The main justification for additional scrutiny of alcohol advertising was that advertisements for alcohol "associate such consumption with happiness, prestige, popularity, and the attainment of a glamorous lifestyle," according to a finding in a bill before the Committee on Energy and Commerce when I testified in 1985. This became known as the justification from "generic deception," that associating alcohol use with good things was inherently misleading and therefore dangerous. These ads not only contain "hidden positive messages" but also "fail to warn of the dangers of alcohol," the argument went.

I think it is safe to say that no advertising wants to convince potential users of a product that using it will make them miserable, unpopular, loathsome, or will get them only a better spot in the gutter. Banning ads on the basis of hidden or deceptive messages would lead to a lot of blank pages in newspapers and silent minutes on electronic media.

A 1977 Supreme Court case, *Carey v. Population Services* ruled that the State of New York could not ban all advertising of contraceptives based on the allegation that it covertly legitimatized sexual activity by minors. I believed that requiring all advertising of alcohol to include statements about the dangers posed by excessive drinking was analogous to that approach to contraceptive ads. Notwithstanding the reality of the health dangers of drunk driving, juvenile alcoholism, and spouse abuse by intoxicated adults, there is little evidence that alcohol *advertising* actually increases any of these dangerous practices; in one study from Michigan State University, scholars found only a 10% increase in alcohol consumption after heavy exposure to ads.

The bill being considered by Congress in 1987 sought to increase the amount of information about the dangers of alcohol and called on alcohol advertisers to supply some of this information. To do so was not in the best interests of the alcohol companies. The Fairness Doctrine required a "reasonable" opportunity for alternative viewpoints to be heard and had been used prior to 1974 to make room for the presentation of alternative views to the advertising claims, but the Federal Communications Commission had ruled in that year that it believed that "standard product commercials" did not trigger the Doctrine because they "make no meaningful contribution toward informing the public on any side of any issue," a view subsequently upheld by a number of federal appeals courts.

The Fairness Doctrine (which has since been repealed) was not an "equal time" rule that mandated precise equivalences of time and space regarding "controversial" matters. This proposed bill stated that no ads would be permitted unless equivalent time was made available for responsible spokespersons to discuss "various adverse effects" of alcohol consumption on individuals and the public. The Communications Office of the United Church of Christ was a prime mover in enactment of the Fairness Doctrine and the ACLU supported it as well.

The exact equivalency approach taken in this legislation would have been extremely costly to alcohol advertisers and might discourage advertising altogether. Moreover, sections of the bill seemed to require licensees to search for respondents and if none could be found, or if anti-alcohol groups refused to produce counter-ads, alcohol ads would not be permitted. This refusal of anti-alcohol groups to produce messages amounted to a kind of "heckler's veto," a long constitutionally forbidden construct that allows persons to violate the speech rights of others by refusing to allow them to speak in the first place.

I warned Congress that the ideas embodied in this legislation would certainly be applied to other products where people claim a health hazard: sugared cereals, automobiles, meat preservatives, laundry detergents, and even eggs. I noted that, if they succeeded in getting this "equal time" legislation, the airwaves might be so full of ads and counter-ads that there might be little space for programming at all. Of course, that would not be upsetting to groups that find rock music programming, sitcoms, and children's cartoons menacing.

When it became clear that these efforts against alcohol ads were not going to make much headway, some of their proponents shifted gears and tried to require warning messages on alcohol products. I testified against some of the suggested warnings in 1990 but indicated that, with some modifications, some of the warnings would pass constitutional muster.

One section of the legislative proposal insisted that any alcohol advertised in the electronic media must include spoken health warnings. The kind of language suggested by other witnesses could consume roughly 7 seconds. The time allotted to commercials was rapidly declining, which meant that a beer company that wanted to run a 15-second ad would have to either reduce its message to 8 seconds or buy a 22-second ad to include the warning and the intended message. It was not so much the added cost to the advertiser but the idea that government would shape the style of the ad that posed the First Amendment problem.

In addition, was the language of the warnings sexist and misleading in its targeting pregnant women, suggesting that their alcohol consumption could cause problems for their unborn children? My argument was that there was no medical evidence to suggest that a single drink by a pregnant woman caused birth defects or fetal alcohol syndrome, although there was evidence that heavy alcohol use by men prior to the pregnancy of their wife could result in low-birth-weight children. I advocated honesty about the health problems for both genders so no constitutional problem would exist.

The effort to regulate or restrict alcohol advertising went nowhere. Perhaps that was because many members of Congress enjoyed their own nip at the end of the day. Congress shifted its attention to restricting advertising of tobacco products with greater success. The liquor industry eventually ended its own self-imposed "ban" on the advertising of hard liquor and today one of the principal advertisers on the popular Steven Colbert late-night show is Crown Royal. The industry ended up adding its own warnings on bottles and cans.

Tobacco

In January of 1964 Surgeon General Luther L. Terry released a monumental study on the health effects of smoking. It linked tobacco use to lung cancer and laryngeal cancer in men, a probable cause of lung cancer in women, and the prime cause of chronic bronchitis in the entire population. One year later Congress passed the Federal Cigarette Labeling and Advertising Act. This legislation, coupled with another law in 1969, required a warning label on most popular tobacco products and barred all advertising in the electronic media. Decades later Congress weighed in on advertising in print media.

I always enjoyed chatting in hearings or elsewhere with the late Oklahoma Democratic Congressman Mike Synar. In the mid-1980s he was the prime proponent of a complete ban on advertising of cigarettes and any other products containing tobacco.

I appeared before the House Committee on Energy and Commerce's Subcommittee on Transportation and Hazardous Materials on many occasions to object to his proposals. Some of the arguments Synar made were quite similar to those made by proponents of the alcohol advertising ban discussed above, but he added the idea that tobacco was a "uniquely harmful product when used as intended." I noted in testimony in 1987 that this notion had "demonstrably more rhetorical than scientific validity" and that I could find no basis for concluding that smoking one cigarette "is more or less harmful than eating one rare steak, even if it's from an Oklahoma cow, or strapping on one hang glider." Even Synar chuckled at the Oklahoma cow reference. Christopher Buckley wrote a novel called *Thank You for Smoking*, in which a tobacco lobbyist tells a Senator from Vermont that he is not sure that smoking is worse than eating a lot of Vermont cheese. I considered it a cute variation on my testimony.

As noted elsewhere, my father-in-law was not a fan of mine. Even after years of marriage, he rarely phoned me to chat. So, I was surprised to get an early morning call from him one day in December 1985. He began, "I have put up with a lot of your opinions, but you have crossed the line now." I asked what he was talking about, and he responded, "You are on the front page of *The New York Times* claiming that banning cigarette ads violates the First Amendment." He was an oncologist and obviously ticked off that I would defend advertising any product linked to cancer of any kind. I mentioned something like "the First Amendment only works if it works for everybody." He was not persuaded and insisted I rethink my view on the matter. I did, concluded I was correct, and never discussed the matter with him again.

Congress stopped thinking it could ban all tobacco advertising, but it began considering the kinds of ads that could be placed in newspapers, magazines, and billboards. In 1965, Congress had passed the Federal Cigarette Labeling and Advertising Act, which specified that states could not impose additional labeling or advertising requirements on cigarettes that carried the Surgeon General warnings. "Warnings" would be placed on every cigarette package, like "Smoking Can Be Hazardous To Your Health." Those warnings became more graphic in subsequent years. I argued that if the federal government removed its pre-emption of warning label advertising, which was also printed as a part of the print ads for these products, it would invite every state to decide what to require be placed on packages and advertising.

Creating some hypotheticals, I suggested that different states would apply different messages. California might insist that one quarter of all advertising copy would have to announce, "Smoking will inhibit your ability to surf"; Ohio might require "The friendly folks of Ohio remind you that smoking makes you less appealing"; and in North Carolina, the add-on language might be "Whatever the Surgeon General thinks, the legislature of North Carolina thinks tobacco will make you healthy, wealthy and wise." I also pointed out that the chairman of the subcommittee, Democrat Tom Lukin of Ohio, had actually said when introducing the bill that he hoped it would lead to more "stringent" warnings in many states.

By 1989, as so often the case, opponents of tobacco advertising began to couch their censorship interest as a way to protect children from the product, naming their new bill the Protect Our Children from Cigarettes Act.

I reminded the Committee that much as they might want to protect children, even the Supreme Court in a case involving dial-a-porn reminded us that, if a ban on any speech is orchestrated based on the observation that it might be seen by children, the entire country is reduced to seeing or reading what is fit for ten-year-olds. As I put it, "Banning cigarette ads if they can be seen by children means ads will be seen almost nowhere except perhaps in topless bars with door guards who can always spot false identification."

That year there was more discussion about the "promotion" of tobacco since the proposed legislation made it unlawful for a tobacco company to sponsor any athletic or artistic event or display the brand of product being sold on cars, boats, animals, or hats and T-shirts. The registered brand name of a tobacco product could no longer be seen in a television show or a motion picture.

Congress also wanted to regulate the few tobacco ads that might slip through the location restrictions. They could not contain any human figure, any scenery, brand name, logo or symbol, or any picture of a product's package, even in front of a neutral background. I noted, "Although everything from cauliflower to condoms can be advertised in a creative way, this bill would make tobacco advertising so bland that it is nearly invisible."

Fundamentally, I argued that companies selling lawful products have the right to create ads and place them where they believe they will be seen by their target audience. "It doesn't take an advertising guru to figure out if you are marketing in a predominantly African American neighborhood, you don't include a model wearing a white hood and a white robe." I rephrased earlier testimony of mine that tobacco advertising has no magic power.

Millions of Americans see ads every day for Kool, Virginia Slims, and Salem cigarettes, ignore those calls no matter how seductive, and never come close to a cigarette vending machine....We remember those Brooke Shields ads where she stuck cigarettes in her ears to show that it wasn't attractive to smoke. We have graffiti artists all over the country who add to the tobacconist's line "Alive With Pleasure" the appendix "And Dead With Cancer."' There should continue to be robust debate about smoking and the consequences of smoking. So long as tobacco products are legal, tobacco companies have a right to make their case in the manner they choose.

Since these efforts to curtail advertising were unsuccessful, New Jersey Democratic Senator Bill Bradley began promoting a way to handle tobacco advertisers by no longer permitting the costs of advertising to be tax deductible business expenses. Clever, but again unconstitutional. As I told *The Wall Street Journal*, "This could become the functional equivalent of a ban on cigarette advertising. It is unconstitutional to burden the speech of only one group of advertisers."

Anyone claiming to be a First Amendment purist should confront the speech that they consider most offensive. That is why the ACLU thought it particularly important that a Jewish attorney in Illinois represent the right of Nazis to march in Skokie, Illinois in 1977. I hate smoking and long championed the elimination of smoking in restaurants when I lived in Northern Virginia. I once told a Congressional committee that I hadn't smoked since I gave up trying cigarettes made from lettuce leaves and "Crooks," wine-soaked small cigars which my own mother wouldn't allow me to smoke in our far-from-smoke-free home. I read a lot of material about smoking and concluded that it was too dangerous an activity for me. In spite of speaking at occasional gatherings of the Tobacco Institute, where cigarettes were in little jars with labels reading "Thanks for Smoking" on the tables, I was never even remotely interested in experimenting with any tobacco products again.

A number of studies examine why children begin to smoke—and the largest predictor of starting to smoke was whether one's family members or close friends do. Advertising ranked low on the list of causes, and even respected health advocates like the former head of the Federal Trade Commission, Michael Pertschuk, concluded in 1983 that, "No one really pretends that advertising is a major determinant of smoking in this country or any other."

The closest a tobacco advertising ban got to enactment was in September 1990 when the House Subcommittee on Health and the Environment approved new restrictions on the promotion of tobacco products. The tobacco industry had enormous clout, although not matching that of the four gun manufacturers who are the principal funders of the National Rifle Association. Many of the provisions in this bill were dropped in recorded votes on the House floor. Some significant provisions remained, including requirements that T-shirts and hats bearing a tobacco product trademark also carry a health warning label, prohibiting the handing out of cigarette samples on public thoroughfares, and changing the size and wording of the health warnings required on packs and boxes of cigarettes. This approach never went any further due to Senate inaction.

My favorite appearance on this topic, though, was at the annual convention of the Kentucky Tobacco Farmers' Association, in Louisville. Designed to be family friendly, many of the male farmers brought with them their spouses and a few children. When I got up to speak, I said, "I want to talk to you today about censorship." I then pulled out the June 1988 (Playmate of the Year) issue of *Playboy.* I could hear some uncomfortable moving in the audience. This discomfort only increased when I opened the magazine, since it seemed obvious that I would be exhibiting the centerfold. It turned to laughter when the audience saw that I was displaying a cardboard pop out insert advertisement featuring the large-snouted cartoon figure "Joe Camel." I did think that starting my presentation this way would ultimately make them uncomfortable even though most of the attendees relied entirely on tobacco for their livelihoods.

Although no ban or serious restriction on the advertising of tobacco products has passed Congress, in 2009 The Family Smoking Prevention and Tobacco Control Act became law. It contained some restrictions on marketing and sales of tobacco products to young people and mandated disclosure of ingredients in those products. The only piece of it that to me raises any possible constitutional issue is the prohibition of sponsorship by tobacco companies of athletic or cultural events. To my knowledge, the ACLU did not weigh in on this matter.

Violence on Television

Also attractive to lawmakers in the late Eighties was finding ways to support a reduction of violence on television. Given the struggle to figure out how to restrict sex depictions, it should come as no surprise that Congress was not about to ban particular images or scenes from being shown on television because they were too gory, or too many people were murdered at the same time. They decided to try to grant an exemption from antitrust laws for television industry companies to meet to "alleviate the negative impact of violence on television." Normally, this kind of meeting would be precisely the kind of coordinated activity the antitrust laws were created to eliminate.

The proponents of this approach claimed that if the antitrust exemption were created, television networks would be able to create a voluntary set of guidelines to reduce depictions of violence. My argument was that, once an industry is told it can all get together and what results are desirable (reduce violent programming), any rules or codes it comes up with are not truly voluntary. Since there are antitrust laws that seem to prohibit such collusion, any exemption that would permit such a gathering but only insofar as it affects "violent" programming should be considered governmental action and thus require intense scrutiny in regard to the First Amendment.

I pointed out that the social science data linking violent programming to actual aggression is slim and certainly doesn't justify this level of Congressional intervention. Depictions of teen suicide had been used to illustrate the causal connection between the small screen and real life. I pointed out that copycat suicides undoubtedly occur, but "there is also very good evidence that when the evening news reports on the suicide of a famous pop singer or a public figure, suicide rates also increase. Indeed, high school use of *Romeo and Juliet* has also been supposed to romanticize teen suicide so much that it causes it. As with sexual material, if the measure of what we should suppress is what one or two people do in response to that speech, then we are all going to be reduced to sitting in a darkened room, presumably without television, in order to prevent some violent image from crossing the eye or the mind of someone who may be affected by it."

After an impassioned speech by Bob Keeshan, Captain Kangaroo to decades of children, I observed that "civil libertarians are parents, too—even parents happy to have grown up with Captain Kangaroo. We know that children of all ages are bombarded with data from the mass media...the constructive way of helping them absorb all this data is through critical viewing, teaching children to analyze and evaluate what is seen on television, and not through the encouragement of television censorship."

The Senate also held a hearing on this antitrust exemption through a bill by Illinois Senator Paul Simon. It was only a three-year period of "exemption." When it passed, I told *TV Guide* that, since it would expire in those few years, "I would heartily recommend that the industry ignore this opportunity" so that it will be "forgotten." The bill had little impact on anything and violence on television increased, leading Simon to threaten even more direct regulation, which never came.

The ACLU did endorse the elimination of some advertising restrictions on other controversial products and services but, as always, there were caveats. A number of members of Congress had proposed a "sense of Congress" resolution to have the Department of Health and Human Services do two things: 1) develop public service announcements on the dangers of AIDS and methods to prevent transmission, and 2) urge television networks to permit the advertising of condoms. Since the former issue, AIDS service announcements, only enhanced the availability of objective information regarding this disease, it did not appear to be an effort to unduly interfere with network programming. This was different than an effort to suggest something more subjective like "more patriotic" programming.

The condom advertising was a bit more problematic. This resolution encouraged the ads "during select adult programming," an unconstitutional effort to restrict the "time, place and manner" of advertising. Second, the resolution seemed to view condoms solely as a method of reducing AIDS transmission and not to acknowledge their use as instruments of family planning, a kind of indicator that contraceptive use of condoms was still taboo.

Political Speech

There were even efforts in Congress to regulate the content of political speech. Everyone understands that incumbent politicians usually want to stay in office as long as possible and thus want to make it more difficult for potential opponents to criticize them. The worst example of proposed legislation in this arena was the Clean Campaign Act sponsored by Missouri Republican Senator John Danforth. The fundamental premise of this legislation was to give any candidate who is the "victim" of a negative advertisement free time to respond, unless that critical ad was aired by the candidate herself or himself and that candidate appeared in the ad. By the late Eighties many television ads were actually paid for and produced by Political Action Committees (PACs), which by law could have no connection with the candidate's team itself. These "independent" ads would most obviously trigger free response time. My one comment most cited by the media was that it was "subtle censorship costumed as good government legislation." Although I have never run for public office, I couldn't imagine, were I a challenger, not wanting to run a negative campaign about all the wrong-headed policies of the incumbent.

In a rare joint appearance, I showed up at a press conference with Terry Dolan of the National Conservative PAC, at the time the most significant rightwing PAC. We both expressed grave First Amendment concerns about Danforth's proposal. I said I understood the sentiments of bill co-sponsor Arizona Senator Barry Goldwater, who had run for President against Lyndon Johnson in 1964. Johnson had been criticized for one notable ad featuring a small child and a nuclear explosion, implying that Goldwater would bring about a nuclear confrontation. Another publication had found dozens of psychiatrists who claimed Goldwater was mentally unfit to serve, a conclusion echoed in later advertising. Consequently, Senator Goldwater was no fan of what he considered negative advertising. He claimed, "dirty advertising has become a business," but that "under the Constitutional right of free speech you can say about anything you want. Frankly, I'm glad that I'm getting out of the damn business." The bill never went anywhere, because even sponsor Danforth conceded during a hearing the same day as our joint press conference that the proposal might be unconstitutional.

Although I had some flirtations with PACs, over the years I have come to see them as a rot on the body politic. The only PACs I support are ones that give the funds directly and immediately to local groups. During the COVID-19 pandemic, I got many unsolicited telephone calls, including one by a woman who was raising funds for breast cancer research. As she droned on, she eventually indicated that she was calling on behalf of a "527 organization" which led me to say, "So you are not raising money to combat a disease; you are raising funds for politicians who you hope will support funding. Not to put too fine a spin on it, I'd say 527s are cancers in the political system."

Without question, the most controversial First Amendment position of the ACLU in the late twentieth century was its approach to efforts to rein in campaign spending. Since I was the First Amendment person there, I was called upon to testify against efforts to curtail spending in elections. Many ACLU members did not accept this argument. This is a truly arcane area of law, but, working with a law professor from New York and an extraordinarily talented legal intern, we did a fine job of taking on the regulators.

As I was leaving the ACLU in 1991, more attempts were made to change the ACLU position. The official view I had espoused was predicated on public financing of primary and general federal elections to create a floor for contributions, while allowing virtually unlimited spending in addition to the public funds. We also opposed granting favorable mailing or broadcast rates only to candidates who operated solely with federal funds, requiring disclosure of the sources of privately funded candidates, and any effort to increase federal funds if a privately funded candidate was successful at raising contributions in excess of what they would have had to adhere to if accepting funds through the public financing system.

At the time, I was generally comfortable with this approach, but I am now far less comfortable with applying such rules to the new collection of funding types that have become a malignancy on the political process: Political Action Committees, 527 groups, and even 501c(4) organizations. All of these had been promoted as "good government" groups helping to clean up campaigning. They failed to do that, and, frankly, since they are creations of Congress, the statutes that created them should be repealed. By 2022, bills were introduced in both the House and Senate to ban for-profit corporations from setting up PACs. These did not come close to passing.

Flag Burning

I confronted other free speech issues during my tenure at the ACLU. One of the most controversial was an amendment to the Constitution which would have prohibited burning the American flag. The Supreme Court had ruled that burning the flag was an act of political speech. The case involved Joey Johnson who had burned a flag at the Republican National Convention in Dallas in 1984 and was promptly arrested. Surprisingly to some, even Justice Antonin Scalia voted to protect his right to burn the flag as a means of political expression. The ACLU legal staff represented Johnson. He was happy to be vindicated, but, when he and three other people burned a flag on the steps of the Capitol to challenge passage of the Flag Protection Act of 1989, it did not result in any arrest, which reportedly angered him greatly. In 1990 that statute was ruled unconstitutional in *Spence v. Washington*.

Since statutes to protect the flag were being declared unconstitutional, an amendment to the Constitution was the only way to secure protection against flag burning. Democratic Senator Alan Dixon of Illinois became a principal sponsor of this effort. He and I were on CNN's *Newsmaker Sunday* a few days after the June 1989 decision. He introduced a constitutional amendment to prohibit the destruction or defacement of an American flag. I noted that the Court had gotten it right because the First Amendment is unnecessary "except for things that are going to be controversial, that are going to get people angry, angry enough to do extraordinary things. What disturbs me is that because of this decision, we suddenly have many in the United States Senate who literally want, next week, to overturn this decision through a Constitutional amendment." Dixon was not the greatest debater and claimed that what flag-burner Johnson had done was like "hollering 'fire' in a crowded theater." When the host, Bob Franken, said that was different from the fire example which involved "public safety," Dixon claimed that it was the same because Johnson could have been assaulted while causing the conflagration.

I pointed out that no one did attack Johnson, in spite of the widespread disdain for his action. "Let's say you make a speech on the floor of the Senate that deeply angers people in Illinois. They shouldn't be able to stop you from speaking because they got angry at what you said, and they certainly should not be able to put you in jail because you caused other people to be angry."

On that same program, Franken asked me if there wasn't something "special" about the flag. I responded that "everybody who wants to censor someone else always finds some reason to claim that whatever they've done is special." I also observed that, in a recent conversation with a Vietnam veteran, he told me, "I didn't risk dying for the flag; I risked dying for the principles behind it, one of which is political opposition and dissent."

Passage of the constitutional amendment seemed likely at first since 97 of the 100 Senators had supported a sense of Congress resolution that the Supreme Court had erred. But, as the scope of the proposal became clearer, more Senators, including some Republicans, balked at voting for it. In October 1989, the vote failed 51-48, falling 15 votes short of the two-thirds of the Senate vote required to send it to the states for ratification. Post-vote I told the press, "Senators demonstrated today that they understand that the right of dissent and the form it takes are fundamental principles of our society." At least, some Senators understood this.

Occasional efforts to revive the anti-flag burning amendment surfaced in later years, but ironically, when Kentucky Senator Mitch McConnell, later the Republican Majority Leader, announced he was opposed to it, much of the steam left the process. This demonstrates part of the old adage that even a broken clock is correct twice a day. In my opinion, McConnell has only been right once.

Hunter Harassment Laws

I met Wayne Pacelle, who was the director of the Humane Society of the United States, when we clashed over the right of Santeria practitioners to kill chickens as part of their religious rituals. I supported their religious freedom to do so, while Wayne wanted to protect the poultry. The day the Supreme Court ruled in favor of the Santeria group, I issued a statement that, "when the claimed constitutional rights of chickens clash with the free exercise right of humans, the people prevail." Wayne had seen that quote in a quick Associated Press story and, when we both arrived at *ABC News* to comment on the decision, noted that he understood why I took that position.

I am an animal rights supporter much of the time, and I invited Wayne to speak on radio talk shows quite often. We discussed how opposed he was to "hunter harassment" laws common in many states that prohibited people from deliberately making noises to scare away game so that hunters wouldn't be able to shoot their intended deer or pheasants. Although there was no Congressional legislation on this issue during my tenure at the ACLU, Wayne asked me to speak to *The New York Times* about it. I said these laws were unconstitutional because "in general, courts abhor the preference of one activity over another...it is pretty hard to prove that protecting the right of hunters is a compelling government interest."

Investigating Religious Controversies

Sometimes I urged that hearings on a subject not occur. For example, in the fall of 1987, the chair of the Oversight Subcommittee of the House Ways and Means Committee, Texas Democrat J.J. Pickle, decided to hold a hearing on federal tax rules applicable to tax-exempt television ministries. This all grew out of a conflict between the evangelists Jim and Tammy Bakker's PTL Ministry and several other prominent evangelists, including the Reverend Jerry Falwell and the Reverend Jimmy Swaggart, who sought to take control of Bakker's empire. Falwell and Swaggart persuaded Pickle to call the hearing.

In a letter I co-signed with Mort Halperin, we objected to this hearing. Our argument was that this was quintessentially a dispute over church polity and theological differences, over what constitutes an appropriate religious ministry. Indeed, this was precisely what ecclesiastical tribunals were designed to address and they shouldn't be scrutinized or second-guessed by Congress. Since there was no claim of unlawful conduct by any of the parties, such a hearing was bound to have a "chilling effect" on religious groups, who would rightly fear that whenever theological disputes spilled over into public view, they would be examined in Congressional "fishing expeditions." Although Pickle did hold a hearing, it focused primarily on the creation of evangelical self-regulation through two multi-ministry watchdog groups.

Speech Codes

Much of what I did at the ACLU was fighting efforts to curtail constitutional rights, but occasionally I was involved in efforts to expand those rights, like when Mitch McConnell opposed a flag burning amendment. I helped anti-abortion Congressman Henry Hyde (R/IL) draft a bill called the Collegiate Speech Protection Act to allow students at colleges and universities to try to overturn college and university speech codes that contained penalties for so-called "hate speech."

During the 1980s, many institutions of higher learning attempted to suppress speech that was accurately viewed as sexist, racist, and homophobic. In 1989, a study by the Carnegie Foundation for the Advancement of Teaching had found that 60% of American colleges and universities had written policies on bigotry, racial harassment, or intimidation, and another 11% were actively working on developing such policies. Hyde's bill was designed to allow students who felt that a "speech code" was interfering with their right to make controversial remarks about gender, race, disability, or other factors to oppose speech codes. It did not protect speech "that was directed at harassment of specific individuals when intended to frighten, coerce, or unreasonably intrude upon them." Nadine Strossen, at the time the Board president of the ACLU, accompanied Hyde at the press conference introducing this bill. She used the example of making threatening telephone calls to a minority student's dorm room as something that could still be punishable.

Hyde's proposal simply made it possible for a student at any college or university that received federal funds to challenge an administration that would "make or enforce any rule subjecting any student to disciplinary sanctions solely on the basis of speech or other communication protected from governmental restriction by the First Amendment." It simply did for speech what the legislation in 1989 had done for sex discrimination: it notified these institutions that if they water at the public trough, there are certain water quality standards they must accept.

I gave a few speeches about this bill and obviously faced pushback. Every speech code I reviewed suffered constitutional defects of both overbreadth and vagueness. The University of Michigan code had just been declared unconstitutional by a federal court for using the phrase "any behavior that stigmatizes or victimizes an individual on the basis of race, ethnicity, religion...or creates an intimidating, hostile, or demeaning environment for educational...." In a nutshell, the code covered too much and was incomprehensible. In Michigan's case, it did not help that one example in a university publication of what was prohibited was a male student stating in a classroom that "women just aren't as good in this field as men," the kind of easily rebuttable proposition which ought to be exposed to the light of day primarily so that it can, vampire-like, rot away.

After I wrote an article for the American Federation of Teachers magazine on the topic of speech codes, a teacher responded that the codes could be acceptable if they were narrow enough and mentioned only specific denigrating words that could not be used. There is a certain appeal to that: "nigger" and "queer" were posited as examples. Don't tell that to Dick Gregory, though, whose autobiography was entitled "*Nigger*," or to Queer Nation, a burgeoning gay and lesbian rights group. In both of those cases, oppressed persons took the language and symbol of the oppressors and recaptured and redefined its use. Even in this narrow formulation, one still would need to look at the intent of the speaker.

Speech can be restricted if it presents a "clear and present danger," and "harassment" and "intimidation" can be barred under some circumstances. We also make it a crime to threaten people, because of the assumption that people frequently do what they say they will. At about this time, a student at Brown University was expelled for shouting racial epithets at night. He could (and almost certainly should) have been disciplined under a neutral principle of no noise above a certain decibel level after a certain hour. Then if he screamed invective or sang "God Bless America," he could have been punished without having to abridge a First Amendment right. Similarly, a group of white male students followed an African American woman student across campus shouting that they had never "had" a black woman. It would not be necessary to construct a speech code to handle this because it was an obvious threat, a direct challenge to the safety and physical integrity of an identified person.

At this time (and, frankly even today), many educational institutions are still racist, homophobic, and sexist. To allow institutions that practice bias themselves to probe the racism or sexism of others is worse than letting the fox into the chicken coop; it's like building a security fence around the barnyard with the fox inside to keep the chickens from getting away. About this time, I had been speaking to the dean of a college who informed me that he didn't think courts were the place to adjudicate what he called "acquaintance rapes" on campus because this was not like "rape by a stranger in an alley." This would come as news to the victim. Frankly, I don't want somebody with such a dim understanding of sexual assault judging whether some student's speech is too sexist or threatening to be allowed to be uttered.

The War on Drugs

The Education Secretary during much of my time at the ACLU was conservative William Bennett. In 1986 he approved of a booklet on how to deal with the drug crisis in American schools, an issue of significance for President and Mrs. Ronald Reagan. Bennett noted, "We have to get tough, and we have to do it now. Because of drugs, our children are failing, suffering and dying." Warren Richey, education writer for *The Christian Science Monitor,* described parts of the booklet as "reading like a manual for countering guerilla warfare in the blackboard jungle." Richey cited this passage. "In some circumstances, the most important tool for controlling drug use is an effective program of drug searches...The effectiveness of ...searches may be improved with the use of specially trained dogs."

My response to this approach was that "American public schools are going to become mini police states. Whatever else they are teaching in those schools, whenever you have widespread surveillance like this, you are also teaching that privacy is not a very important value in schools. And that is an unsavory lesson to be teaching our children." My friend Arnold Fege, then an executive with the National PTA and a former innercity principal, also warned, "What we don't want to do is turn schools into fortresses, because if there is anything that disturbs the learning environment it is a fortress mentality."

I occasionally debated Secretary Bennett. One morning we were on separate segments of the local Fox news. The studio was in the far end of Washington. In the morning, it was difficult to hail a cab to get back to my office. Bennett drove past me on the curb, stopped his car and offered me a ride. I accepted and then started rummaging around in the console between our seats. "What are you doing?" he asked. I said, "Just checking that you don't have any cigarettes here." He laughed because he had recently gotten into some trouble as the "anti-drug" czar when he conceded that he was still a smoker. I didn't find any Marlboros.

The Palestine Information Office

Political speech by controversial non-U.S. entities was also on my agenda, particularly when Reagan's State Department ordered the Palestine Information Office (PIO) in Washington to shut down in the fall of 1984. The theory in this situation was that the PIO was financed by the Palestine Liberation Organization (PLO), which the Department noted was affiliated with terrorism. At the time, *The Los Angeles Times* and other editorial boards pointed out that this move, although unconstitutional, was at least better than a Congressional effort underway to force the closing of the PLO's United Nations mission in New York City. Even the Secretary of State, George Shultz, noted that he felt he had the authority to take this action against a "foreign mission," but that it would have limited practical effects since the PIO could simply be reorganized and refinanced by U.S. citizens.

I told a crowded press conference that this whole effort was a "naked assault" on freedom of speech because the only function of the PIO was to disseminate information about the activities of Palestinians and to have employees give speeches about the cause around the country. There was no claim of any unlawful conduct or even any failure to regularly report under the Foreign Missions Act. I continued, "The PIO has a right to speak even if the great majority of people in this nation find what they say offensive or wrong...Advocacy of political positions is by all measures one of the vital interests protected by the First Amendment and the State Department's posture in this matter is incomprehensible."

I met with Arab Americans and some progressive Jews to consider legal action against the State Department. Eventually, efforts to close the Office were deemed unconstitutional in several legal proceedings.

Film Censorship without Bans?

The Library of Congress now runs a national Film Preservation Board. It was created in 1988 by an act of Congress permitting a thirteen-member board to select up to twenty-five films each year to be included in a National Film Registry "as an enduring part of our national cultural heritage." Once a film is selected, it cannot be distributed or exhibited in a format "materially altered" or "colorized" (if in black and white) unless it contains a notice or warning label that the film has been changed from its original and that "certain creative contributors did not participate in this version of the film." It would have passed sooner but for my years of effort to stop it by providing a legal basis for the objections of the Motion Picture Association, then headed by Jack Valenti.

Although its principal supporter was Senator Paul Simon, Democrat of Illinois and a fine member of Congress, it didn't pass both houses of Congress until the Directors Guild sent actor Jimmy Stewart back to Washington. Stewart was most notably in DC in a famous black and white film, *Mr. Smith Goes to Washington.* Stewart convinced Congress that this Board was essential to the preservation of what is good in American cinematic culture. Despite my many chats with Senator Simon about this, he remained intransigent and, with the help of Jimmy Stewart, won.

This was not a modest proposal like having a group of bureaucrats select which paintings should be hung in the National Gallery nor even which films should be purchased for restoration by the American Film Institute. This Board was making decisions based on the content of the films to select which are an enduring part of the culture and then treating those films differently from all other motion pictures through mandatory labeling. Whether such a disclosure is seen as a "benefit" (as it is by some film directors) or a "burden" (as seen by many copyright owners), imposing it based on a governmental assessment of content should be constitutionally forbidden.

Some, including Senator Simon and his House counterpart, Democrat Sidney Yates of Illinois, claimed it amounted to nothing more than "truth in advertising." In my view, even this characterization is not one the First Amendment permits. Could the government require that a newspaper print the names of all of its stockholders on the front page once a week? Could a government board watch every movie before its release and require that it contain a few frames at the beginning noting whether it has a happy or sad ending? Even if those postings were truthful, they would violate the principle that governments cannot compel a person to say what the government thinks those individuals should say. The Supreme Court has ruled that no one can be forced to carry "Live Free or Die" on her New Hampshire license plate or be forced to recite the Pledge of Allegiance. One should not be able to force a copyright holder to inform the public that changes were made in the original version. There had even been celebrated cases involving the labeling of certain foreign documentaries as "political propaganda," though even the Justice Department never took the position that an exhibitor couldn't take the labels off before exhibiting the films.

In some circumstances courts permit the government to force people to speak or not speak government approved words, like "I do" in marriage ceremonies. Since there is a genuine need to preserve public health or safety, you cannot cry "Fire" in a crowded theater. Since when, though, is watching a colorized version of *The Maltese Falcon* bad for your eyes? You can't prohibit colorizing the film on the grounds of public safety.

The original version passed was even worse, since it allowed for the Board to craft a process for removing films from the Registry. How can the "enduring...national cultural heritage" change so that it would ever be appropriate to remove a film? Doesn't this just encourage highly charged and subjective disputes between Board members with differing theories or ideologies about cinema? This elitist selection process did not even permit average citizens to make suggestions about what should be included.

My suggestion in one op-ed was that "the best thing that could happen to the Film Preservation Board is for it to be preserved somewhere in a 'Hall of Bad Ideas.'" These films keep getting selected each year, but I remain unconvinced that the First Amendment is served when a cable service can't run a modified film without a label or a projectionist sends the audience home if the film print is missing its proper label.

Although the bill was adopted in 1988 as described, by 1991, when it was up for re-authorization, Congress wisely terminated the labeling requirement.

Moral Rights and Jury Nullification

I always regretted that some of my efforts to enlarge ACLU policy never made it through the official process to be adopted as policy. For example, I pushed rejection of the Berne Convention and the entire rubric of "moral rights," and I pushed the ACLU to strongly affirm jury nullification.

The Berne Convention has been adopted by many European nations and includes several provisions antithetical to the First Amendment in the United States. The Convention discusses three "rights" for an author of a work of art: the right to claim authorship of the work (not a problem), the "right to object to any distortion, mutilation or other modification" of the work, and the right to object to "other derogatory action in relation to the said work which could be prejudicial to his honor or reputation." These rights are to be enforced by provisions in the legislation of any country where protection is sought.

United States law does not recognize these latter two approaches to regulation of content, believing that contract law should resolve most matters in this arena. A book's author, for example, can restrict a person assigned a copyright for their work from using it in another medium or from "modernizing" the language in the book. There have been a few cases, as with the *Tarzan* novels of Edgar Rice Burroughs, where this was permitted. Efforts to block use of one piece of art in conjunction with another are almost always unsuccessful. For example, Dmitri Shostakovich sued Twentieth Century Fox for incorporating some of his classical music in an "anticommunist" film whose premise he disagreed with. He lost.

I had hoped that the ACLU would oppose outright any and all efforts to restrict the use of a piece of art whose ownership is transferred without contractual restrictions. Otherwise, a writer might object to having his text illustrated with photographs taken by someone he does not favor, claiming that the juxtaposition is "prejudicial to his honor" or a cinematographer or director might sue to enjoin "colorization" of a film by the copyright owner, arguing that computerized coloring is "mutilation." This reasoning would allow courts to get involved in all manner of artistic disputes. For example, in Spain a production of *Don Quixote* was stopped by the courts which determined that the actors were miscast.

I chaired an ACLU Committee twice during my tenure on the Board following my employment there, but the strong voices of "preservationists" on these panels made any policy change impossible. I would hope that if someone purchased the "Mona Lisa," they wouldn't want to draw a mustache on her enigmatic countenance, but I think that new owner has an absolute right to do so. It is the seller's responsibility to include in the sales contract that no modification of the work is permitted.

The second issue I wish the ACLU had embraced was the doctrine of "jury nullification." This is an idea with roots in English common law. A jury is permitted to ignore both the facts of a case and the law as explained by the judge if that jury does not believe the law is itself appropriate. It was a doctrine that was advertised by anti-draft organizations both toward the end of the Vietnam War and during the Carter Selective Service registration. It has been practiced mostly in marijuana possession and obscenity cases. There are no cases where a judge has been asked to explain this doctrine and has done so. This is hardly surprising. One man in Oregon was prosecuted for distributing leaflets about nullification outside an Oregon courthouse.

However, in a subsequent appeal, the court found that his explaining the idea without referencing any specific case was protected by the First Amendment.

AIDS

Mort Halperin and most of the other staff at the ACLU knew that the spread of AIDS and HIV would raise enormous civil liberties issues in the mid-Eighties and beyond. Until the hiring of the extraordinarily talented Chai Feldblum to work on this issue in Washington, I did a few months of work to try to focus legislators on the real dangers of discriminatory treatment of persons with HIV/AIDS. Feldblum went on to be a professor at the Georgetown University Law Center and was appointed to the Equal Employment Opportunity Commission by President Barack Obama. Because the ACLU developed new policy positions slowly, the early months of the epidemic left me with little to say based on direct policy of the ACLU.

For one of the only times in my career, I actually had to tell the writer of a November 1985 article, "Our organization is still wrestling with some pieces of this debate." In the beginnings of this disease, there were proposals to quarantine those affected and to engage in sweeping testing of persons in schools and businesses. Conservative Congressman William Dannemeyer (R/CA) had introduced five bills on the subject, all of which were so draconian that it did not take new ACLU policy to oppose them. Dannemeyer's proposals included prohibiting persons from working in the healthcare field if they had HIV infections (he conceded this would require testing), cutting federal funds from any city that didn't close its bathhouses (he insisted this was not "anti-gay"), and a "sense of Congress" resolution that infected children should not be able to attend public schools.

In 1988, Surgeon General C. Everett Koop had proposed mass AIDS screenings on a major urban university campus and comparable testing in a number of high schools. At the conclusion of the first international AIDS summit in London, Koop indicated that since students of this age were among the most sexually active in the country, it was important to understand the prevalence of HIV and

AIDS. Koop said that all students would be tested at the still unchosen university and that the process would be "done out in the open, above board; everyone knows that the blood specimen is not in any way tagged." He later envisioned a "one day, open-air campus gala" on AIDS prevention. The Surgeon General also indicated that results of the testing would simply be aggregated for research purposes and not be made available to the individual test subjects. Student groups expressed reservations about this mass testing, questioning whether anonymity could be guaranteed. My colleague at the ACLU legal department in New York, William Rubenstein, told *The Washington Times* that any testing would need to be "anonymous and voluntary, with strong informed-consent provisions." I was skeptical that Koop could guarantee any of these three conditions.

I was invited to dinner with Democratic Congressman Steve Solarz of New York, along with right-wing activist Richard Viguerie, to discuss early Congressional response. When the topic of pre-marital AIDS testing came up and Solarz thought it was obviously needed, I pushed back and said, "Congressman, you act like a positive test would just cause a cancellation of the wedding. It is much bigger than that: if you cancel the wedding and try to conceal why, rumors will leak out, and you have just ruined someone's life." At the time, the diagnosis of AIDS was a death sentence for almost all who received it, but the prognosis was improving and there were persons who actually survived the infection. That "ruined life" might go on for a long time.

Major cities were also experimenting with bleach distribution programs where outreach workers would go on the streets to so-called "shooting galleries," where addicts often shared needles, and hand out bleach and instructions to clean needles with it. Although hardly a panacea, when combined with increased voluntary testing, it was widely hailed as a step in the right direction. Predictably, rightwing activists criticized this this as another step toward encouraging "needle exchange" programs and drug use. Even the District of Columbia's Public Health Commissioner Reed V. Tuckson opposed that step as sending an "inappropriate message at a critical time in the history of our city." Though having clean needles available has some risks, I never thought that those were more substantial than the benefits of limiting the spread of HIV among persons living with addiction.

From the very different vantage point of decades later, I recall how confused the debate on AIDS was for the first few years, the hysteria, and how deadly the diagnosis was. Some of the medical issues were similar to those raised in the early months of COVID-19: Would the virus mutate quickly? Would physical barriers like condoms and masks actually effectively curtail the spread of the virus? What is the point of "tracking" individuals with HIV since there was at that time no treatment for it?

During my research for this book, I found three pages of notes on yellow lined paper for a presentation on AIDS and HIV. My notes were hopelessly naïve, although they raised many of the civil liberties issues that would be litigated in earnest over the next decade. The military had begun to test all new recruits and later, all active-duty personnel, claiming that transmission could occur by persons working closely together in places like armored tanks or with battlefield blood transfusions. Employers were seeking ways to assess whether would-be employees had HIV and under what if any circumstances employees could be terminated. From dealing with other illnesses, the country had some standard restrictions in employment law for adverse treatment based on disabilities. Courts generally viewed customer preference and increases in health insurance costs as invalid justifications for firing a disabled person. Similarly, the mere appearance of impairment could not serve as the basis for adverse job treatment.

Outside of these policy questions came other practical matters. Although it was useful for people to be tested and told their status if they wanted to know, how could the country do a serious public education campaign about this sexually or body-fluid-exchange transmitted disease at a time that sodomy laws (and drug use laws) were present in most of the nation and criminalization of sodomy had recently been upheld by the Supreme Court? Sodomy laws were not finally declared unconstitutional by the Supreme Court until 2003 in *Lawrence v. Kansas*–twenty years after AIDS showed up. It would be difficult to even explain modes of transmission in a meaningful way. Film star Rock Hudson came down with AIDS early in the crisis and his lover attempted to sue Hudson's doctor for knowing that Hudson was his partner and not informing him or public health authorities that Hudson had AIDS. Privacy and civil liability questions were everywhere.

The AIDS debate struck nerves in every section of the country and throughout every profession and institution. Realtors in Houston, Texas, were being pressured to advise clients if a house for sale had been previously occupied by a person with AIDS, while California realtors were prohibited by law from disclosing such information. Radford, Virginia, schools barred the Cornerstone Theater Company from performing in its schools because its members had acknowledged that it had previously performed for AIDS patients. The ever-anti-gay Senator Jesse Helms got an amendment passed on a 94-2 vote that required any AIDS education materials to stress "abstinence from sexual activity outside of a monogamous marriage including abstinence from homosexual sexual activities." This vote came after Helms' staff found a sexually explicit comic book published by the Gay Men's Health Crisis of New York City which Helms claimed depicted "sodomy" and didn't encourage a change in such behavior. The comic had not been directly funded by the federal government. When Helms showed it to President Reagan, he "slammed his fist into the desk in outrage." A more moderate ban replaced Helms' ban a few years later. In 1991, the Centers for Disease Control issued far more permissive rules, which CDC officials said would still not give AIDS educators "license to do things that are wildly explicit." What that meant was never made clear.

School Prayer, Equal Access, Secular Humanism, Child Care, Government Sermons, and Religious Displays

My experience with the ACLU brought me close to the center of important church/state debates that I later pursued for twenty-five years with Americans United for Separation of Church and State. The very first day I worked for the ACLU was a rainy Monday. I went out to the "swamp" surrounding the Capitol to make comments to the press about the start of a Senate debate on Ronald Reagan's proposed Constitutional amendment to return organized prayer to public schools. I imagined that someone watching who hated the

ACLU must be thinking, "Look at that jerk. He doesn't even have the common sense to come in out of the rain."

That evening I emceed a gathering on the Capitol steps featuring many religious leaders, all expressing opposition to the amendment. As I was introducing the speakers, I explained that prayers were so complex that almost any of them would offend some people: "The only prayer acceptable to every religious person begins with 'Dear' and ends with 'Amen.' Anything in between becomes a problem." *USA TODAY* printed that remark, but omitted my observation that, for non-believers, even the "amen" would be controversial.

This amendment had clear majority support, but a constitutional amendment requires a two-thirds vote of both houses of Congress. When the debate began, a significant number of Members were undecided. President Reagan directly lobbied many Senators but was generally not successful in obtaining their support for the amendment. For me the most important Senators who came out against its passage were Republicans Barry Goldwater of Arizona and Arlen Specter of Pennsylvania. Goldwater concluded that in Arizona among Native Americans, so many differing religious views would make it "impossible to come up with a meaningful prayer for everyone." Specter actually went to the White House to meet with Reagan and told the President how much pain he had felt as a lonely Jewish student amid overwhelmingly Christian majorities where he grew up in Kansas.

The debate went on for two and a half weeks. In the end, the vote on March 20, 1984, was eleven votes short of passage, spelling the defeat of the measure and effectively foreclosing its return to the floor in that Congress. Unfortunately, the fight to bring organized religion to public schools was far from over. Enter The Equal Access Act.

This proposal was co-authored by Congressman Don Bonker (D/WA) and Carl Perkins (D/KY) and was originally drafted to guarantee that students could use public schools for voluntary meetings during non-class hours even if the meetings were about religion and included prayers. Proponents claimed that this was necessary to uphold the free speech rights of students and was just a modest extension of a 1981 Supreme Court case called *Widmar v. Vincent,* in which a majority of the court ruled that facilities on public university campuses must be open to sectarian student clubs. This sounded good to hundreds of House members, and I told the *Congressional Quarterly* that the bill had a 95% chance of passage, even though the ACLU and other groups opposed it. First Amendment supporter Congressman Don Edwards (D/CA) launched a month-long parliamentary effort to delay the bill's consideration in order to build opposition to a bill he said would "interject the imperial power of the federal government in Washington, DC, into every one of the 15,517 school districts in the United States." He correctly noted passage of this amendment would permit "outside preachers, priests, rabbis, cult leaders and gurus" to conduct worship services in public schools if invited by students to do so.

Bonker had drafted his original bill in a form that would allow it to bypass the Judiciary Committee and be evaluated solely by the Education and Labor Committee, chaired by bill supporter Perkins. Edwards' redraft was sent to his Judiciary Committee where Edwards held a hearing on the bill at which I and others testified in opposition to it. I said that Bonker's bill was a "wolf in sheep's clothing—special privilege legislation for religious speech masquerading as equality," a sentiment Edwards wrote me was "beautiful." It soon became clear that Speaker of the House Thomas P. "Tip" O'Neill, Jr. (D/MA) and Rules Committee Chair Claude Pepper (D/FL) opposed the measure, and it would likely not be cleared for a House vote.

The weeks of dueling hearings led to some interesting tactics. Although I often supported the rights of new religious movements to proselytize in public spaces, I did a joint press conference with Jackie Speier, a staff member of Congressman Leo Ryan who had been killed during a trip to Guyana to visit the Reverend Jim Jones' Peoples Temple. She had testified in favor of more scrutiny of so-called "cults" at the unproductive special hearing on cults that I had criticized during my tenure at the United Church of Christ. However, we agreed that, notwithstanding that big disagreement, we could unite in our opposition to any religious groups getting special access to public schools. Our press conference prompted Don Bonker to issue a "Dear Colleague" letter with a cartoon labeled "Sophistry, American Style." It depicted Phyllis Schlafly, a conservative, anti-feminist activist and lawyer, saying that, "If the ERA becomes law, men and women will be forced to share bathrooms" and a guy (looking suspiciously like me) saying, "If Congress allows student-run religious groups, our schools will be overrun by holy rollers and Moonies." I wouldn't have used that kind of language of course. In case Bonker's cartoon was misunderstood, he added, "The measure will not allow ritualistic slaughter of animals or services using poisonous snakes."

One of the most annoying aspects of Bonker's approach was his claim that his bill was "necessary because constitutional rights are being denied to students who want any kind of religious activity." This was patently false, because the idea of America's public schools as test-tube growth venues for all free expression aside from religion was ludicrous. The bill was brought up under a process that was rarely used on controversial matters called "suspension," which on Monday afternoons, permitted bills to come to the floor with no amendments allowed, and required a two-thirds vote for approval. He tried, but the 270-151 vote was 11 votes short of passage. Was this dead now? Most observers said "yes" but the Senate sponsor Jeremiah Denton (R/AL) and the principal outside advocate Sam Ericcson of the Christian Legal Society had other ideas.

Jeremiah Denton was a former POW in Vietnam and was obsessed with helping the Religious Right with its legislative agenda. He had originally intended to attach a Senate version of Bonker's bill to an important math and science authorization, but, in those more polite times in the Senate, the fact that the bill's principal Senate opponent, Lowell Weicker (R/CT), was on official business in France at the time led the leadership to postpone the vote. Upon Weicker's return, the bill was brought to the floor. I was in Weicker's office meeting with his chief of staff that afternoon when the Senator walked in and said, "Let's negotiate; we are meeting with Mark Hatfield in a few minutes."

So we met: Hatfield, Weicker, the two staff members from their offices, and me. And we negotiated. Weicker asked Hatfield why it was so important to protect only *religious* student group meetings and not *all* student meetings. Hatfield had no problem with the more inclusive language, and I floated wording that I had discussed with Ericcson. If the school had created a "limited public forum" at which student groups could meet, all student speech at those meetings that had "religious, political, philosophical or other content" would be protected. Hatfield also agreed to other changes: federal funds would not be cut if a school did violate these meeting rights, no school officials could attend unless necessary for insurance purposes, no limitation on the size of the group (to eliminate the possibility that small or unpopular groups would be prohibited), and no direction, control, or regular attendance by outside figures. The next day, Weicker's staff person called me and said, "So if you are ever trying to avoid being executed, who do want to defend you—Weicker or Hatfield?"

I had already gotten the support of the ACLU's Washington Office Acting Director Morton Halperin and Executive Director Ira Glasser in New York to agree to be neutral on this bill if these changes were made. Ira told me this would have been a dream students' rights bill back during Vietnam. Weicker said, even with the changes, he couldn't vote for it, but he wouldn't filibuster it either. I did warn the press that even this version would "lead to decades of litigation," which, of course, it did. People tried, with mixed success, to claim that the bill permitted posting religious announcements on school bulletin boards, and that any time a student did not have a class scheduled was "non-instructional time" when religious meetings could take place, notwithstanding that the statute specifically defined it as "before or after actual instruction" occurs. The bill also allowed for chaplains to come to lunch meetings to "share the faith." At the end of the deliberations, Weicker said "even if the ACLU finds this acceptable, I don't and will not vote for it." He didn't and a handful of other Senators voted against it as well. These included Republican John Danforth of Missouri, an Episcopal priest, who, as usual, weighed in too late in the process to make a difference but argued that it is the nature of religious groups to proselytize and "protections" in the bill against this were unlikely to stop that impulse. It passed overwhelmingly.

Although I was happy to make the case for why the ACLU had not opposed this bill and did so in the group's quarterly newspaper, at the ACLU biennial meeting a year later, there was (per the ACLU's rules) a vote on whether to try to overturn the law in court. The ACLU did not pursue this, but the decision was challenged by others, and the ACLU filed a "friend of the court" brief in support of the school system. The Supreme Court ruled in 1999 in favor of a student who sued a school for denying a religious club the right to meet, in *Westside Community Schools v. Mergens*: religious clubs could meet on the same basis as other student clubs.

The law became the basis for the dramatic increase in Gay/Straight Student Alliances all over the country, and, to its (rare) credit, the Religious Right in general was willing to accept its use for that purpose. Some Religious Right figures had opposed its final passage, viewing it as a "Trojan horse" that would allow for "anti-family, anti-neighborhood, anti-values" groups to promote the idea that "anything goes." There were efforts to challenge its use for "gay clubs" but all but one of those challenges (one in Texas) were unsuccessful.

Senator Jesse Helms (R/NC) was nothing if not persistent. After failing to pass legislation to return government-sponsored prayer to public schools and ban all abortions, he concocted an effort to remove jurisdiction from federal courts to consider certain topics, like prayer and abortion. The Supreme Court in 1985, in *Wallace v. Jaffree,* found that an Alabama statute for prayer and meditation was unconstitutional. The Court had looked at the legislative history of the statute and found that all of its advocates spoke about prayer and nobody discussed meditation. The Court concluded that this statute was really a ruse to return government promoted prayer to public schools. Jerry Falwell wrote that he had sleepless nights after this decision and called Helms who told him this denial of jurisdiction, referred to as "court stripping" was a way to circumvent bad Supreme Court decisions and would only take a simple majority. Helms did get it to a vote in September of 1985, but it was defeated on a 62-36 vote to table the measure. Even "Mr. Conservative" Senator Barry Goldwater announced he was "embarrassed" to have originally endorsed this approach. Most major newspapers had editorialized that this short-circuiting of the Constitution was itself unconstitutional with the *Washington Post* noting directly that this was not to modify the responsibilities of federal courts, "but to change constitutional law." This strategy was abandoned soon thereafter.

Fast forward to 2020. By the time the COVID pandemic abated, and students were gradually returning to public schools, the Right began to focus on the preposterous claim that something called "Critical Race Theory" was being foisted on schoolchildren. This mirrored a battle the Right started in the late 1970s and 1980s about how "secular humanism" was rampant in public schools, an idea widely promoted by Eagle Forum head (and the woman widely and accurately credited with derailing the Equal Rights Amendment) Phyllis Schlafly, assisted by Senator Orrin Hatch (R/UT) and Lynne Cheney, head of the National Endowment for the Humanities from 1986 to 1992 and mother of Liz Cheney (R/WY). In 1978, Hatch had added an amendment to an education bill that required that parents be given access to all instructional materials "used in connection with any research or experimental program or project." It also noted that "no student shall be required...to submit to psychiatric examination, testing or treatment...in which the primary purpose is to reveal information concerning a variety of topics including 'political affiliation, sexual behavior, mental and psychological problems potentially embarrassing to the student or that student's family, income or critical appraisals of other individuals who have close family relationships with the student.'" In 1984, Hatch additionally got passed an amendment to the Education for Economic Security Act which authorized magnet-school assistance for the following two years but prohibited use of any funds for "courses of instruction the substance of which is secular humanism," a construct not even defined in the legislation. Department of Education regulations followed, however, which made it slightly clearer what was being proposed.

Major education organizations, including the National Education Association and the National School Boards Association, had serious reservations about the implementation of both of these bills, and one of the sister organizations of the ACLU, People for The American Way (PFAW), did more direct work on this than the ACLU. The ACLU had been conducting a multi-year study on the teaching of values in public schools to assess whether it was possible to do so without promoting religious viewpoints.

PFAW had filed a lawsuit in Greenville, Tennessee, before I joined the ACLU to object to the censorship of a wide swath of teaching materials in a school district. Rather than directly bar use of certain materials, the lawsuit objected to the requirement that failure to provide alternative reading matter to that found objectionable by some fundamentalist Christian parents constituted an infringement on religious freedom. Its President, Anthony Podesta, noted that parents in seventeen states had sent form letters to their children's school districts objecting to classroom activities citing the "Hatch amendments." These letters demanded that their children not be involved in such activities as "biofeedback," "transcendental meditation," "role reversal," "open-ended discussion," and similar programs and activities. PFAW also held a major day-long conference on the subject of "Values, Pluralism & Public Education" at the National Press Club in April 1987. I spoke at that event.

When all the criticisms of these measures were assessed, it was clear to me that Phyllis Schlafly and her supporting organizations knew exactly what they would do with all these regulations: stretch their meaning to be maximumly destructive of educational policy in local schools. After all, they wanted to do away with public schools entirely.

The American Association of School Administrators held a national convention every year. In 1986, it was held in Washington, DC. They organized a debate between me and Phyllis on the subject of values in schools. AASA is hardly a radical group of educators, but Phyllis laid into the educational advocacy groups like they were a pack of demons, insulting virtually everyone in the ballroom and not seeming to try to persuade any moderates among the audience that she might be making some good points.

I started my twenty-minute presentation that followed Ms. Schlafly's this way, "I had a dream last night. The Eagle Forum and the ACLU agreed about something—and the Earth stopped spinning. Well, in light of the last 20 minutes, it is apparent that the cessation of rotation is not going to happen." I pointed out that Pat Robertson, then contemplating running for the Presidency (which he did), was at least honest in discussing what he meant when he talked about "moral values" in the schools, "There can be no education without morality and no lasting morality without religion," he had said.

Ms. Schlafly charged that schools which were not actively promoting anti-Christian values were trying to be "values neutral," which she considered nearly as dangerous. I began by pointing out that there are all kinds of commonly shared moral values being promoted in schools and that most of these weren't remotely controversial. What was controversial was defining the line between right and wrong. This could be communicated by what is said or by how the school administration treats its students. The broad latitude in allowing schools to choose curricular material is central to good pedagogical treatments, "Every judgment call is not a violation of someone's constitutional rights. Throwing out a worn-out book is not censorship."

I said we should all abhor "viewpoint discrimination" where it occurs. There are obviously certain manageable principles that can be brought to bear on things like book selection for school libraries. Is the book age appropriate? *The Kinsey Report* doesn't need to be in elementary schools. Is the book well-researched and well-written? Is it current? Does it duplicate the content or viewpoint of other books in the library?

On the other hand, I noted, "Some judgments...particularly when a decision is made to remove a piece of material solely because of the ideas it expresses or the manner in which it expresses them" are troubling to some. Those judgments are suspect. I gave examples of the kinds of books being challenged or even banned because of content: Lakeland, Florida, *The Supernatural*; Jefferson County, Colorado, *Greek Mythology*; Shippensburg, Pennsylvania, John Knowles' novel about adolescence, *A Separate Peace*; and others. And "Let us not forget the fights over Shel Silverstein's *A Light in the Attic* in Beloit, Wisconsin, a book whose crime is "encouraging children to break dishes so they don't have to dry them." There is no definitive decision by the Supreme Court on permissible limits for removing books, but a plurality decision in 1982's *Island Trees Union School District v. Pico* suggests that if a decision to remove a book is designed "to contract the spectrum of available knowledge," it would represent an unconstitutional effort toward the "official suppression of ideas."

I was critical of Ms. Schlafly's "back to basics" education approach, which she had defined as an alternative to the "anti-parent mishmash of social-problems discussion that fills many public school hours today." She also encouraged schools to raise the question, "Does it lead the child to believe that government spending programs are the formula for economic prosperity, instead of hard work and perseverance? Does it lead the child to believe that disarmament rather than defense can prevent a future war?" It seemed to me that her objection was not to the coverage of social problems, so long as the resolutions were in line with her political ideology. As with today's debate over how to deal with racism discussions, it seems absurd to give no consideration to slavery or the theft of Native Americans' land and destruction of their cultures or to consider economics without looking at the values behind capitalism, socialism, or the federal income tax.

Schlafly was also a supporter of "don't teach certain subjects"— excluding honest discussion of things like sexuality (surely teenagers would not think of sex if there wasn't a class on it) or teen suicide. "Of course, students are affected by what they see. Earlier that year in Japan a famous pop singer committed suicide and within weeks over a dozen teenagers had copied that conduct, leaving behind evidence that they linked their decision to the singer's own death. We can't really ban television from reporting what has happened. We could, though, try to help students understand what the news means to them," I countered.

Phyllis had just issued a "Students' Bill of Rights," which was bizarre. One was the "right" to be taught English in the first grade and be transferred to "intensive phonics" if that student couldn't read by the middle of her or his first year. Another "right" was to "privacy," which sounded good, but actually stated that, "schoolchildren cannot be forced to discuss or play Magic Circle or keep journals about attitudes and feelings." A third guaranteed the right to religious faith, which included not having to do assignments or engage in classroom activities that denigrate that faith, "teach witchcraft," or teach that "there are many gods." Of course, schools can't promote paganism any more than they can Presbyterianism, and mentioning something cannot be equated with promoting it. Indeed, religion's role in history can be taught and the Bible can clearly be present in a school library.

She was also critical of something called the "Lifeboat" game, an exercise where the teacher posits that there are ten people in a boat that will not be rescued for several days, and the food supply will only be sufficient for six of them. I used this exercise with high school students and there was always a breakthrough moment after students figured out ways to judge the value of each occupant or setting up lotteries to decide who lives when someone would say, "It is better to risk that all die because killing is always wrong." According to her this exercise violated the "right" of students to maintain their own moral values. And Schlafly's "rights" went on and on. The "right" to "be inspired by classroom lessons, not depressed or disturbed," the "right" not to be told that parents are old-fashioned or might abuse you, which seemed to deny that there was an epidemic of child abuse or that a third of the child pornography out there was produced by family members.

I also criticized her work on the federal legislation mentioned earlier and her publication of a book, *Child Abuse in the Classroom,* which was her edited version of the many hearings around the country. I blamed her for the dramatic expansion of the Hatch amendment's meaning and purpose and the inevitable effect of slowing the dissemination of information to students all over the country.

I concluded my remarks with the proposal that students often learn more about values from the conduct of school officials than from anything in the formal curriculum.

Moral issues will always arise in public schools. The real question is whether the schools will fulfill the task of helping train future voters and leaders to think seriously about the issues that will shape their futures. It is a goal that will not be achieved unless those who run the schools reject sectarianism, intolerance and censorship while traveling the roads of robust inquiry and recognizing that the way they treat the students may itself be sending the strongest "moral" lessons those students will learn.

Of all the issues at the ACLU, the one we "lost" that bothered me the most was how to fund childcare for pre-school children. This provided a sad example of how dangerous it can be when progressives fight each other and third parties. In this case, young children and their parents became victims of those internal fights. By the early Eighties, childcare was clearly in crisis. There were too few places that preschoolers could go to get safe and affordable care while their parent or parents worked. In general, any federal approach to helping deal with this was met with hostility by the Religious Right. James

Dobson weighed in against "Uncle Sam plunging headlong into the babysitting business, inevitably forcing Christian childcare facilities out of business through unfair competition and punishing mothers who elected to stay home with their families."

One would think that with this kind of blunt rightwing opposition, progressives would have been able to fight back and get something done. Unfortunately, that did not happen. There was a major battle over the role, if any, that religious institutions would play in providing federally funded childcare.

As this effort was beginning, Congressman Pat Williams (D/MT) saw me in the hall and asked me to respond to an idea he had: why not open public schools early and keep them open late to accommodate the needs of parents? To me, this was a brilliant idea: community-based childcare at existing sites, which would also help employ more teachers. As Williams talked to more progressives, the idea was really catching on with the strong support of the National Education Association and the PTA. This proposal did not rule out participation by non-school entities but insisted on some strong church/state protections if any federal funds were involved: no use of those funds in any activity that "advanced or promoted religion," no funds for capital improvements, a requirement that religious symbols or icons be covered up, and a guarantee that there would be no discrimination based on religious affiliation in admissions or in the employment of providers.

Pat Williams was a unique figure and the only member of the House who actually returned to live in his home district following an electoral defeat in 1997. Most stayed to become lobbyists. Pat helped direct the Center for the Rocky Mountain West. I had lunch with him when I was making a speaking tour of Montana. (His cousin was Robert "Evel" Knievel, the legendary daredevil who used to ride motorcycles to jump over long strings of motor vehicles and even the Snake River Canyon.)

Unfortunately, his idea did not have the support of a real civil rights icon, Marian Wright Edelman, who had long led the Children's Defense Fund in Washington. She was dead set against this approach. In one memo in the summer of 1988, she wrote, "It's really sad when we were expecting to be fighting Falwell and Schlafly that we are fighting the NEA." The NEA called this accusation "nonsense" when "childcare is an urgent need." She was a strong supporter of something referred to as the ABC bill (the Act for Better Childcare Services), which was a slight variation on the same bill that had died in 1988. She was concerned that "her babies" as she would refer to children in need of childcare, would be best served if religiously based providers were included as recipients of federal dollars. In a conversation with Mort Halperin and myself and in a subsequent memo on the subject, she said that church/state issues should be left for resolution by "regulatory bodies and the courts." I didn't trust the courts, and I trust them less today.

A bill finally passed in 1989. This bill prohibited a commission on health and safety standards to set more stringent standards than the strictest existing state standards and prohibited those standards from being imposed on any childcare providers who were not receiving federal funds. It provided an insurance pool for liability insurance, and explicitly permitted grandparents and other close relatives to receive federal funding.

I am consistently disturbed that the one real chance to provide responsible childcare for all children was derailed by someone as generally sensitive to children's needs as Marian Wright Edelman. In 2022, childcare is still an underfunded mess and public schools are rarely used for such assistance. There is no federal mandate to use public schools this way, so the practice is rare. This was a golden opportunity derailed almost entirely by one progressive activist.

The Reagan years were filled with efforts to interject religion into political campaigns. I battled each one. In August 1984, while campaigning in Dallas, Texas, Reagan told the audience of 12,000 that "The truth is that politics and morality are inseparable. And as morality's foundation is religion, religion and politics are necessarily related." This was his consistent message, that only religion can generate morality, something I disagreed with fundamentally.

Senator Paul Laxalt of Nevada served as Reagan's campaign chief in 1984 as Reagan was seeking re-election. In summer 1984, he wrote a letter to 45,000 pastors in sixteen states asking them to assist in voter registration. It read in part, "Dear Christian Leader...join with us to help assure that those in your ministry will have a voice in the upcoming elections...a voice that will surely help secure the reelection of President Reagan and Vice President Bush...we cannot afford to resign ourselves to idle neutrality in an election that will confirm or silence the President who has worked so diligently on your behalf and on behalf of all Americans."

I told *The Los Angeles Times* that this "shows a remarkable disrespect for religious diversity because it so clearly focuses on the 'he is one of us' attitude...that the only people who are fit to be President are those people with traditional values." The deputy press secretary for the Reagan-Bush '84 campaign responded that this was just a "nonpartisan effort to enlist ministers to try to register voters in their churches." I found it hard to keep a straight face at this preposterous description of the intent of the Laxalt's letter, particularly when the press aide conceded that the letter was sent to ministers only in states where the election contest with Democrat Walter Mondale might be close.

There was yet another controversial mailing in 1985: sermons sent by the Department of Health and Human Services (HHS) to religious leaders to promote the idea of adoption. How religious were these sermons? One included the comment, "How blessed we are to have been chosen before the world was made to become adopted children through Jesus Christ...Let us open our minds and hearts to our Christian and community responsibility and restore these children to their rightful place within the family."

HHS described this as just a "casual thing." My comment to the reporter at UPI who discovered this was that, "the government cannot be in the sermon-writing business any more than it can be in the prayer-writing business for any or all faiths." My future communications director at Americans United for Separation of Church and State, Joe Conn, also weighed in, "The ministers are perfectly capable of preparing their own sermons without help from Uncle Sam." Unfortunately, we could not think of a way to litigate this issue, but, to my knowledge, this "sermon distribution" was not done again.

Another Reagan era decision after his re-election in l984 was to have the National Park Service reinstate a Nativity scene in the annual

Christmas Pageant of Peace on the Ellipse near the White House, a decision reversing twelve years without it. Jack Fish, the National Capital Regional Director of the Park Service, had determined that the recent decision by the Supreme Court, *Lynch v. Donnelly,* upholding a creche scene in Pawtucket, Rhode Island, which included some secular images like candy canes and dancing bears, permitted the nativity scene. The Ellipse display was paid for privately at a cost of roughly $3,500 and included nearly life-size wooden figures of Mary, Joseph, and the baby Jesus along with the three wise men, two angels, sheep, a donkey, and a cow.

I was sent to the Ellipse the day it was installed to give comments to the press watching it being set up. Even I was shocked at the ludicrous appearance of the display of the Nativity scene. It was enclosed in a wire mesh cage sandwiched between a cage of live reindeer and a display of a Yule Log, which I told the press looked like a "Christmas zoo." In testimony the following year, I urged the creche be removed from that year's pageant. I described this scene and said, "Rarely was Justice Hugo Black's admonition so starkly in evidence—'the union of government and religion tends to...degrade religion.'" The most prominent advocate for the return of the creche, Anne Neamon of the group Citizens for God and Country, was upset. She told *The Washington Post* that, "They have been decorating the [national Christmas] tree with a six-pointed star, which is the Star of David, instead of the five-pointed star, which is the Christian star."

When governments leave the secular sphere and enter the realm of theology, they should know that many people will not be happy. My colleague Sally Greenberg of the Anti-Defamation League, in her testimony on this matter, noted that this display of a central symbol of Christianity in a federal display made Jews and members of other religious minorities "feel like isolated, second-class citizens" and that the idea of adding more religious symbols would certainly bring a "war of the symbols." This was a government-sponsored event and not a genuine "open forum" where all could display their symbols.

Across the country for decades after this kerfuffle, the number of Christian symbols erected on lawns in front of or in roads leading to the doors of government buildings proliferated. I joked citizens would not be able to get through them to pay their parking tickets.

On one curious note, there was a single time when I agreed with Senator Jesse Helms about a church/state matter. The ACLU and the Senator opposed the naming of anyone to be ambassador to the "Holy See" in Rome. Worse than having an official representation to the fictional city-state of the Vatican, this provides a diplomatic liaison directly to a religious denomination, as bad a policy as naming an ambassador to the Presbyterian Church or the Church of Scientology. On the day of the final Senate vote that named William Wilson as that ambassador, I was in a Senate elevator alone with Helms. He knew who I was from our many disagreements, but I just smiled and thanked him for voting against having an ambassador to the Vatican. He smiled back.

Chapter 3

ANOTHER ROAD TAKEN—OUR SECOND CHILD

Many parents who have a great first child wonder about having more children: Will the first child do well with a brother or sister? Will we have the energy to start raising another child? If we are thinking of another child, is it to balance the gender of child number one? We had all those questions, but we figured Christina would do fine, we had the energy, and we really did want another child. After seven years, we had Nicholas Lynn and couldn't have been happier. Nick preferred that I not include more of his story in my memoirs.

It's left versus right every weekday on...

BATTLELINE

...with today's news makers in the middle.

On the left: Barry Lynn

Barry Lynn is "that liberal lawyer who represents witches, pornographers, and draft dodgers."

And civil rights activists and environmentalists, too. Barry passionately believes the right of free speech should be just that-- free. And he has dedicated his life to making sure that mis-guided people don't stomp on that right.

During his years with the ACLU, Barry went head-to-head with some powerful interests. And he's still doing it. He's not afraid of stepping on some toes. Or getting his own toes stepped on.

On the right: Peter Flaherty & Bob Grant

Peter Flaherty & Dr. Robert G. Grant, who also know a thing or two about verbal combat, alternate as co-hosts.

Peter is Chairman of the Conservative Campaign Fund, and he directed Citizens for Reagan. He raised money for the contras in Nicaragua, and helped unseat former House Speaker Jim Wright. And he was the first to file legal action against the check bouncers on Capitol Hill.

Bob is President of the American Freedom Coalition, bringing together people of all colors, religions, occupations and political backgrounds to promote family values. He is also Chairman of the 350,000 member Christian Voice-- the nation's oldest and largest Christian lobby. He's Chairman of the Board of the Coalition for Religious Freedom, founded to protect our first amendment freedoms.

WEEKDAYS • 3-5 PM ET • INDEPENDENT BROADCASTERS NETWORK
INFO: 813-573-4402 • FAX: 813-573-3501

Barry Lynn's later rendition of Battleline, a spirited discussion of the politics of the day on radio.

Chapter 4

IF I RUN FOR PRESIDENT,
I WILL SKIP NEW HAMPSHIRE

Joanne and I both felt emotionally exhausted. Washington was just too draining a place. Perhaps we ought to look for a respite in a smaller, more manageable city, or even in a rural area which had some proximity to intellectual and cultural activities. I thought that the talents I had developed in Washington could be transferred to a state or local level and that, with some flexibility, they could be turned to the good use of promoting peace, justice, or constitutional principles.

When my radio career with NTR came to a crashing halt in one of Pat Robertson's major financial failures (could it have been what he called my "satanic" presence?), I had already announced my resignation from the ACLU. It seemed the signs were all pointing us out of town. As a mid-career, rising-star physician, I knew Joanne would find it easier to get a job than I would, but I was optimistic that there was some place that would want both of us.

That place turned out to be Dartmouth College Medical Center in Hanover, New Hampshire. What would a nice lawyer/minister be doing at a medical center? I was recruited to work on publicizing and popularizing a relatively new way to think about medical care in the United States. As the Clinton era was to begin, many innovators in medicine thought that the time was perfect to have a dramatic change in health care delivery. Those folks had not yet met "Harry and Louise," the denizens of a remarkably effective television ad against the Clinton health care reform initiative, nor had they realized that Hillary Clinton herself would be leading the Sisyphean charge.

The work I was to do was in Dartmouth's Center for Evaluative Clinical Sciences (CECS). The basic premise of this group was that there were great differences in the use of certain medical innovations, like hospitalization itself, differences which seemed more related to the existence of capacity (available hospital beds) than to actual evidence that hospitalization improved the outcome of care. Dr. Jack Wennberg, for whom I worked, had done classic research comparing hospital stays in New Haven, Connecticut, and Boston, Massachusetts, for lower back pain. Boston physicians more frequently prescribed hospitalization. There were more hospital beds in Boston than in New Haven. It turns out that there was no data to suggest that the more frequent hospitalizations helped you do better. Wennberg called for "outcomes-based research": Before we expended funds for a procedure or intervention, we should know that it improved the outcome for the patient.

At some level, this is so painfully obvious, it is hard to believe it wasn't already the cornerstone of modern medical practice. In the real world, hospitals with empty beds lose money, and prescription medicines are costly to develop. The use of over-the-counter remedies can put drug company executives on the fast track to lifestyle downsizing. With the U.S. health care system's costs spiraling, knowing what actually works better than more expensive alternatives seemed a message that both consumer advocacy liberals and fiscal conservatives could rally around.

I decided to go to Dartmouth right after Christmas and get immersed in this new world while waiting for Joanne and the children to come up after the school year was over. We took a U-Haul of stuff up to a rented townhouse in Vermont, just over the border from Hanover, New Hampshire. We were to arrive on a Friday morning. I was incredibly impressed that the local cable television people said they would get someone there to install cable at noon that day. We arrived at 11:30, the installer at noon. Where else in America does the cable guy come on time? I had already figured out that television was going to be important on the cold, lonely nights in the bleak mid-winter that I was told would last until the end of April and then be displaced by two weeks of "mud season."

Joanne went back to Washington, but my first few days were spent communing with Jack Wennberg and his wife Corky and with a genuinely nice couple, Hal Schwartz and Ann Flood, who had been recruited to start at the Center that very week. I went to another physician's home on a lake, seasonally frozen, and learned about ice fishing. Cutting a hole in the ice, placing a tent over the hole, and actually catching fish attracted to the bait dropped through the hole was an interesting way to spend some time.

My first workday was that Monday. I arrived to find that my office was in a college dormitory that had been converted to office space a few years earlier. The walls were the gray of almost every dorm room in America; you could tell exactly where the beds would have been placed and smell the beer spilled in the glorious aftermath of a night of collegiate partying. The place was a dump.

As I was unpacking my few books and filling out some forms, Jack came to the door and asked if I knew anything about intellectual property law. I acknowledged that I had a little background, but it was limited. He said he'd still like me to join him at a meeting starting in minutes with the lawyers for Dartmouth College over some copyright issues he was trying to work out in dealing with the Sony Corporation. Sony was to produce a series of "interactive videodiscs" dealing with patient choices for intervention. They hoped these would be used for a growing number of medical conditions. I knew very little about this project and wondered who had even gotten this contract to this point.

I met with the lawyers, tried reading the contract as the meeting opened. I could see that Jack primarily wanted to maintain control over the content of the discs and be able to use his best scientific judgment about revisions and additions. Frankly, I don't remember much of what the College's lawyers wanted to protect for Dartmouth. They were affable but didn't seem wildly competent. I made a few comments, each based on some rule of law I remembered from addressing copyright matters and the First Amendment at the ACLU. It was not a hostile engagement. It just seemed odd to be in a meeting so late in the process of dealing with a multinational corporation with scads of expert lawyers and feel that so many basic details were still on the table. And why would pulling me in at the last-minute help?

The afternoon was spent primarily meeting other members of the CECS team and reading some of the work the team had already prepared that looked at other medical interventions. I also met the fellow who had actually produced the interactive videodiscs. When I first saw him, he looked familiar. It turned out he had, until recently, been the medical correspondent for CNN television. Like myself, he had left the hectic pace of the big city to settle in the rustic north. He seemed to be a hard-working fellow.

I found myself wondering if these people really liked each other. Did they feel like a team? Since no one invited me to dinner, I headed to downtown Hanover for food at one of its half-dozen restaurants and for a couple of VHS rentals at the only video store. My instincts told me there would be a lot of days and nights on my own. I got back to Vermont and settled in at the television.

Then the phone rang. It was Joanne. "How was your first day?" I could tell that this wasn't just the standard and obvious question about anyone's first day at a new job. This was a question of weight and moment. I said, "It was a little strange. People seemed colder than I expected. Jack seems not to quite know what I'm doing. I'm not as clear about what my job here is." She paused and asked, "Are we making a mistake going up there?" I rejected my instincts and said, "I'm sure things will feel better." I should have been painfully honest. I should have said, "I've never been so sure we made a mistake." I would regret that decision for years.

One Sunday evening in early July, after Joanne and our children had moved to Hanover, we had a 4th of July dinner with my Dartmouth boss and some visiting professors interested in outcomes research. Later, I went to bed and developed increasingly severe stomach-area pains. Joanne told me it was undoubtedly from some food we had eaten, perhaps one of the dips that had been left out in the sun too long. Joanne had left to sleep on the sofa because of my insufferable whining. I had a more ominous sense that something was seriously wrong. Two more hours and I decided to crawl out of bed (I couldn't stand up by myself) and wake Joanne. She could tell I had a high fever and helped me into the back seat of the car where I could stretch out and moan while she drove to the emergency room.

My fever was so high that I can barely remember what happened there. My only clear recollection was the phrase "pancreatic cancer" before I was given anesthesia. When I finally awakened, I was incredibly relieved to find out that the cancer diagnosis had been wrong. I "merely" had a seriously infected, ready-to-burst appendix. I would spend the next six days in the hospital—but it was not the end of my appendix as it turned out.

While in the hospital, I learned firsthand just how unresponsive the medical profession can be to patients' need for information and their wishes. I had a series of roommates, the most seriously ill a Vietnam veteran who was about to have his third limb amputated. He was in severe pain. When he wasn't crying or screaming, he had his television blaring on MTV so loud that I couldn't sleep. Doctors and nurses would come in and tell me I should sleep more. I thought it should be obvious why I wasn't. I didn't blame my roommate. I just couldn't figure out why they didn't move me to another room if sleep was so important.

To deal with the severe headaches that had developed post-operation, the doctors tried a variety of pharmaceuticals. None of them did much for the pain, but all of them made me nauseous or so spaced out that I was having poorly formed hallucinations. I knew what I needed: a drug called Darvocet, a big pink painkiller I had used for decades for severe headaches that had no effect other than stopping the pain. They seemed insulted that I would even suggest that I knew what was best for my pain; they told me they didn't even stock the drug. I responded that, under the assumption that the two things I needed to sleep were a quieter room and a pink pill, they ought to either find both or send me home where I could locate both. Eventually, I got another room, I got my Darvocet, I got sleep, and I got to go home. I was on antibiotics while recovering, doing some work, and hosting a radio show for a few hours each afternoon.

The Fourth of July is about the time that interns start their hospital rotations. They may or may not be fully prepared for the patient care they are about to deliver. My appendix was removed in Hanover, New Hampshire, and two weeks later when I got back to Washington, I was having dinner in a Northern Virginia restaurant when the plate seemed to rotate in front of me. A member of the wait staff noticed that I was not looking too pert and called an ambulance. Joanne was in Denver, and I asked my longtime friend Peter Broida to come with me to the hospital, which he did. The emergency room staff found a massive infection in my abdomen, and I was put on a regimen of twice daily self-induced infusions of antibiotics into a catheter in my arm. As this process was beginning, I recall asking what would happen if this scheme did not work to curtail the infection and was told, "You would die because we could not operate on your body due to the infection." Honest, yes; pleasant to hear, resounding *NO*. I did recover with appreciation for this modern medical miracle called antibiotics.

Things did not get any better at Dartmouth as the months progressed. Before Joanne and the children moved to Hanover, I was returning to Washington for long weekends every few weeks, often via a train from White River Junction, Vermont, which had a sleeping car. At some point, I had developed an intense reluctance to fly. Trips on the plane from New England were tortuous events of anxiety thanks to the worst forms of weather. We hit turbulence during one winter storm and experienced three separate lightning strikes on the plane. Rationally I know that lightning hitting a plane is not a serious matter because the plane is not grounded. There will be no electrocuted passengers. When I described this incident to a pilot the next day, he assured me that I was right about the grounding, but then added that in a storm so concentrated, "the winds were probably the thing the pilot was worried about." Now I had even more to worry about. In another snowstorm, the plane had to abort a landing in Manchester because the runway access was obscured with blowing snow. Don't they have autopilot landings for this? Indeed, didn't I fly back to Dulles airport just weeks earlier and have the pilot announce that this flight was designated as the monthly test of automatic landing? Why announce something like this in the first place?

We still had our house near Washington, so we had to make trips back and forth for work or house care even after Joanne and the kids–and the horse and my mother–moved to New Hampshire.

These flights seemed to symbolize the generally rocky path at Dartmouth. Jack Wennberg had great hope that his whole approach to medical system reform would get a great boost from Dartmouth's efforts, ultimately successful, to get former Surgeon General Dr. C. Everett Koop to join the faculty of their medical school. I had two past run-ins with Koop earlier in my career. First, I opposed his nomination as the U.S. Surgeon General because of his anti-choice views. Second, and much more directly, as previously discussed, I challenged his efforts to regulate, or even ban, advertisements of tobacco products. Although I am a rabid anti-smoker, and I agree with every regulation of the habit of smoking, I firmly felt that as long as the country considered this a lawful product, people should be able to learn about it through advertising. I had mentioned these disputes to Jack even before taking the job, but he assured me that this would not hamper me working with him. Ironically, Koop's son happened to be a visiting professor in the history department of a nearby college, so Jack arranged a few meetings with him to discuss the forthcoming Koop Institute and how we would all work together as one big happy family. Koop's son also assured me that my history with his father would not be a problem for the future.

Perhaps the son never talked to the father. By late spring, Koop had announced to the Dean of the Medical School that he would under no circumstances work with me, ever, and he would not come to Dartmouth if I worked there. He noted that "word on the street in Washington is that Barry Lynn is in the hip pocket of the tobacco industry." My first response was to be indignant and begin to research my First Amendment advocacy on this matter. My few presentations to the Tobacco Institute were just unpaid efforts to figure out strategy to defeat Congressional ad bans. I even told the head of the Institute that I didn't think the sign near the podium where I was speaking at some event, "Thank You for Smoking," was a very effective marketing device. My pockets were hardly filled with tobacco-stained lucre.

I passed this information on to Jack and even had a telephone conversation with the Dean, suggesting that perhaps he should have called me to check out the veracity of the allegations being made about me by Dr. Koop, their new faculty hire. It just seemed that the truth ought to carry some independent weight. It didn't. I doubt that the Dean ever followed up with Koop, who agreed to come to Dartmouth, conditioned on my having no relationship with him and not being employed by the College. Jack had assured me that we would move forward on our transformation of the health care system with me as a consultant. This vague role did not appeal to me.

The outcome? The U.S. health care system was hardly affected by the thoughts of the Dartmouth researchers; Koop's Institute was largely managed long distance from Washington, since apparently even Koop was bored in Hanover; the Dean was gone within a year; and the videodisc project was abandoned by Sony even before the advent of the DVD made the clunky technology of laserdiscs a museum artifact.

Jack Wennberg's approach to almost everything appeared to me to guarantee failure. He would go 90% of the way down a road (as in the Sony deal), see the giant lemonade stand at the end of the trip, and then suddenly decide that he should (just possibly) have been on another road from the start. The last 10% of the road was going to feel very long, if it was traveled at all. It felt to me that he considered most of his staff incompetent. His maddening style of management led to a thoroughly unpleasant job experience. I resigned.

Chapter 5

PEOPLE WHO HAVE SHAPED MY WORK

The World's Greatest Deliberative Body…on Occasion

The United States Senate was called "the world's greatest deliberative body" by President James Buchanan. Given that Buchanan has generally been considered one of this country's worst chief executives, perhaps he can be forgiven for not recognizing incompetence when he saw it. The first time I recall being aware of the Senate was while on vacation with my parents in Ocean City, New Jersey, and watching the debate over the Tonkin Gulf incident on a big television set in the Hotel Lincoln's activities room. I didn't know anything about the people speaking, but most of them seemed convinced that a military response was justified due to the claimed attack on two American naval vessels. A few Senators objected to giving the President broad authority to respond indefinitely but no one questioned whether the incident had actually happened. Years later, of course, it became clear that it had not. So much for the "great" deliberations that night.

My recollection of a number of United States Senators runs the gamut from a few powerful moral leaders to some grand disappointments and some genuinely bad people. I'll just hit the highlights—and lowlights—here. I've already told stories of Senators Phil Hart and Bob Dole, and I've mentioned others in telling stories of my work. Here, I'll elaborate on a few more with some novel interactions.

I first met Senator Ted Kennedy (D/MA) when I worked for the United Church of Christ, at a meeting to develop strategies for granting statehood and two Senators and an actual voting Representative to the District of Columbia. There were many squabbles about tactics and timing. Then Senator Kennedy swept into the room. He listened for a while and made an astonishing off-the-cuff speech about the injustice of three quarters of a million people, residents of the District of Columbia, paying taxes and sending their children to war without having their interests represented in Congress.

Ted Kennedy attracted staff who were incredibly loyal and stayed in their jobs for many years, including the son of Supreme Court justice Thurgood Marshall. They saw what they were doing as public service and not just a steppingstone to a cushy lobbyist job. Some staff wanted to protect him from getting endlessly involved in controversial causes people would bring to his attention, but he would often ignore their caution and note that "someone" would have to do it and he was that "someone." Later, after I became director of Americans United for Separation of Church and State, we were celebrating our Fiftieth Anniversary. Kennedy was out of town and could not attend. He insisted on taping a message for our dinner attendees. He began: "For fifty years, Americans United has been a skillful, tireless and indispensable ally in the ongoing struggle to protect religious liberty." He then observed that if Americans United had not made it clear in 1960 that religion was not supposed to play a role in selecting a President "my brother might never have been elected."

His abiding committment to our issues and principles was as important to me as any policy he supported or speech he gave.

Rick Santorum is one of the dimmest bulbs I encountered in the Senate. However, he is not without a certain charm. He is one of the few Republicans in recent Presidential campaigns who did not say God told him to run or that the Almighty had made it clear he was the chosen one. Rick did always say that his wife Karen was told by God that her husband would become President.

Santorum (R/PA) and I battled over religion and public policy. He was one of the biggest boosters of President G.W. Bush's Faith-Based Initiative that doled out grant money to religious groups allegedly doing good work in the community. But the money came with no significant strings attached to prevent discriminatory hiring practices and efforts to proselytize. Santorum was also responsible for putting language in an appropriations bill that he thought could bar the teaching of evolution in public schools, or at least mandate the inclusion of so-called "alternative theories of creation."

My mother-in-law, a staunchly conservative Fox News devotee who lived in Western Pennsylvania, loved Santorum. She was about to celebrate her 90th birthday in 2012. A few days before the festivities, I was observing a rightwing religious conclave sponsored by the Family Research Council and Santorum was one of the main speakers. I ran into Mrs. Santorum a few hours later, introduced myself and said: "Your husband and I are often at odds, but my mother-in-law is a big fan. She is a constituent and having her 90th birthday on Sunday. I wonder if I could get the Senator to sign a card for her." She replied that she would make that happen and had me come see the two of them later that afternoon when he would be finishing an interview with Sean Hannity. I went to find a suitable card in the hotel's gift shop.

I watched the end of the soft-ball interview with Hannity and then sat down with the Senator. Santorum asked me to give him a few facts about my mother-in-law so he could personalize a message for her. I mentioned that she was one of the first women to attend medical school during World War II and that her work as a radiologist in Western Pennsylvania had led to the naming of an imaging center for breast cancer screenings after her at a hospital in Indiana, Pennsylvania. He wrote a very nice note incorporating these ideas on the inside of the card I had purchased.

When the writing and signing was over, I mentioned: "My advice, Senator, is that you always look at the front of the card before you sign anything inside. Now, you know that I am a straight shooter, so this image of the White House is where my mother-in-law wants you to live, even though I don't." Mrs. Santorum chuckled and said: "Barry, what would it take for you to come over to our side?" I responded: "Probably the end of human history."

Santorum was a major player in getting conservative judges appointed to the federal bench. He made one mistake in those appointments, though, by pushing for John E. Jones to serve in the Middle District of Pennsylvania. Jones was assigned the case in which Americans United and the Pennsylvania affiliate of the ACLU challenged a school district for promoting "creation science" as an alternative to evolution. Jones' blistering decision against the school system remains one of the most comprehensive repudiations of junk science in history and put an end to promotions of "creation science" for several decades.

Santorum left the Senate, repeatedly ran for the Republican Presidential nomination, became a CNN commentator, and formed a movie company, Echolight Studios, to make "Christian worldview" films. The first was a major box office flop, *The Christmas Candle*. It generated lots of expensive advertising and plenty of terrible reviews. Santorum and the company decided to go another route for motion picture number two called *One Generation Away*, as in, we are only one generation away from losing our freedom. The film was promoted almost exclusively to mega-churches that have their own major audio and video setups. The company also asked if I would be in the movie. The director and film crew showed up at the AU offices, two cameras and (at my insistence) a make-up artist in tow.

I was acutely aware that it is always possible to edit a film in a devious way in which parts of sentences are strung together with material in between left out, a kind of visual ellipsis. Just to take notes, I asked Sarah Jones from our communications department to sit in and observe. It would have been great if I had been offered a meatier role: an aging Batman, the inventor of a cure for cancer, or even a heroic (and aging) rescuer for someone tied to train tracks. But all I got was the role of "me."

The film was first screened at the conservative Heritage Foundation. When Santorum was asked by an attendee after the showing why he had people like me in the movie, he replied that he was sorry there weren't more comments by people like me because he found them so frightening. Who would have guessed that anything I said would be so scary?

Then there is South Carolina Republican Senator Lindsey Graham. My only serious encounter with Graham was when he was still in the House but seeking to move up in the political world. ESPN had a few shows about the intersection of sports and policy. One Sunday in 2000,

Lindsey and I were scheduled to appear to discuss the Supreme Court decision earlier in the week *(Santa Fe Independent School District v Doe)* that ruled 6-3 that a Texas school district could not loan out its public address system to students to offer a prayer before the games.

Graham was predictably horrified by this decision and said: "I think we are going to see a lot of people standing up in football stadiums over the next few weeks and offering the Lord's Prayer out loud." I replied, "That might happen, but I'd like to think that you as an elected official would try to get people to understand what the Court said instead of essentially telling them how to thumb their noses at the decision." I suggested he be a little more creative: train a flock of parrots to recite the Lord's Prayer and then release them over high school stadiums before each game.

I don't think Mr. Graham liked me after that and am reasonably confident he didn't like me before either.

Barbara Boxer (D/CA) presented a different challenge. Senator Boxer was a strong civil rights advocate and champion of reproductive choice. My sole significant encounter with her, however, was not a pleasant one.

One of the projects done by fourth grade students in California each year until 2017 was to recreate, using popsicle sticks or sugar cubes, the twenty-one Eighteenth and Nineteenth Century Spanish missions along the Pacific coast. These had great religious significance historically, but, to be historically honest, they were also the sites of conflict and forced labor by indigenous people. Some of those missions are not in great repair and a bill was proposed to fund their reconstruction, a bill Senator Boxer strongly supported.

The Republicans on the Senate Interior's Subcommittee on National Parks, Recreation and Public Lands Committee didn't want to give Senator Boxer a victory on this funding proposal and developed a sudden interest in exploring the constitutionality of such money going to religious buildings, which in many cases were still used by actively worshipping congregations. They called me to see if I would testify. I knew that they had impure motives but that, as a matter of law and policy, they were correct.

I wrote and delivered testimony that made it clear that if you couldn't use government funds to build religious edifices, you also couldn't spend government money to fix them. Senator Boxer sat in stony silence in the back of the hearing room, shaking her head at much of what I said. It was clear to many of my colleagues that she was furious.

Shortly after the testimony, Americans United was approached by a couple who had asked to use one of the missions for their wedding. Most of the missions are theoretically available for rental for personal events including weddings. However, the mission they wanted to use said "no" because only one of the couple was a Catholic. This was so discriminatory that Americans United filed a lawsuit on their behalf. Unfortunately, it was dismissed for technical reasons. However, seeking funds from the government while engaging in discriminatory practices, clearly violates the Constitution.

Congressional Knuckleheads

Much of the time I was at Americans United, Republicans were in charge of one or both houses of Congress. The House leadership was encrusted with characters such as Newt Gingrich of Georgia, Ohio's Dennis Hastert of Illinois, and John Boehner of Ohio. Gingrich was best known for his Contract with America, a multi-pronged effort to pass ultraconservative restructuring of government. Religious conservatives wanted more red meat. And the Christian Coalition's Ralph Reed and others pushed Gingrich to take up their Contract with the American Family, which he did, but with less success.

In 1995, one of Gingrich's top staff members was quoted as noting that his boss rarely went to church but "thinks religiously." Upon his re-election as Speaker of the House in 1997, Gingrich insisted that until Members "learn in a nonsectarian way–not Baptist, not Catholic, not Jewish...to reestablish the authority that we are endowed by our Creator [with],...[and] seek divine guidance in what we are doing, we are not going to solve this country's problems." I recall writing him a letter at the time inquiring how you establish the authority of a "non-sectarian" deity, since pesky theological disagreements have led to centuries of schisms and produced over 1,500 religious groups currently in the United States alone. In my unanswered letter, I also wondered why he had claimed after the 1996 elections that America must be "submissive to God's will" and insisted that "This country will never again be healthy if we don't have the courage to confront the spiritual and cultural and moral deficit that is an even greater threat to our future than the economic deficit." I'm all for ethical thinking but any spiritual deficit we have is best addressed by the religious community and not by politicians, particularly Gingrich who, among other things, divorced one of his wives while she was in a hospital struggling against cancer, and while he was "dating" his next wife. Gingrich and his third wife, Calista, produced a book about all the religious statements and images in Washington, DC, buildings and occasionally invited pseudo-historian David Barton to address members of Congress and present his slideshow that purportedly demonstrated that the separation of church and state was largely mythological.

Gingrich resigned from Congress in 1998 and was followed, ever so briefly, by Congressman Bob Livingston of Louisiana, until he too was forced to concede an extramarital affair, telling his colleagues that he had "strayed from my marriage." Next in line was Illinois' Dennis Hastert, a former wrestling coach and a member with a 100% correct voting record from the Christian Coalition, supporting a school prayer amendment, private school vouchers, every anti-abortion proposal ever considered, and a defunding of the National Endowment for the Arts because it had funded art that offended people.

Hastert met with Cardinal Francis George in Chicago shortly after becoming Speaker to discuss how to aid Chicago's ailing Catholic school system. As he put it, "When we talk about education, we talk about education of all children, public and private." This was a typically fallacious comparison. The Constitution guarantees us freedom of speech but doesn't require that the government buy us each a computer or a printing press. Similarly, the Supreme Court squarely decided in 1925 that religious groups can set up their own school systems, but it had never held that all taxpayers must help fund those alternatives to public schools.

Hastert, too, had to resign as Speaker following a conviction for evading banking reporting requirements when he was paying hush money to boys he admitted to sexually assaulting when he was a high school wrestling coach.

By 2011, the Speaker was John Boehner (R/OH), now better known for his television commercials promoting his support for commercial marijuana sales and a book, written during the pandemic, in which he criticized Fox News. He would never have done either during his tenure in Congress. Indeed, as one of his first acts as Speaker, he decided that the complete text of the Constitution would be read aloud in the House chamber, a stunt that was to be a prelude to requiring all proposed bills to contain a reference to the section of the Constitution that grants Congress the right to enact such legislation.

This "reference" idea may sound useful, but it mistakenly assumes that everything in the Constitution has an obvious meaning. I wrote in *The Washington Post* that "The Framers of the Constitution knew they were writing a document for the ages. Many of the provisions, as many judges have pointed out, are 'majestic generalities'" to be interpreted by courts.

Tom DeLay (R/TX) never became Speaker of the House, but he did serve as Majority Leader of that body. He didn't like me, but I was shocked when a writer for *The Washington Post*, doing a magazine profile of him, called me one afternoon to inquire why he hated me so much. The journalist said he seemed "obsessed" with me, claiming every time he tried to pass "good" legislation, "Barry Lynn stopped it." Somebody thought I was a power player? However, in true Washington fashion, the *Post* writer said, "I wanted to talk to you because frankly I've never heard of you." From wheeler-dealer to complete unknown in one phone call!

Why did DeLay give me this credit? Perhaps because of an embarrassing position I put him in during the controversy over Ms. Terri Schiavo who had finally been allowed to die in 2005 after nearly fifteen years in a persistent vegetative state following cardiac arrest. Her husband Michael attempted to have her artificial feeding tube removed on several occasions, presenting evidence that she would not have wanted to have her body maintained in this state of complete unawareness. Her parents disputed this claim and fought him in court. The case had been appealed over twenty times since an initial determination by a Florida probate judge that there was "clear and convincing evidence" that Ms. Schiavo had communicated her wishes before her heart attack and fall that she would not want to be kept alive with machines. Some of these appeals were to federal courts, which had uniformly rejected any need to intervene in what were quintessentially state matters. DeLay supported the parents.

One Saturday, a group of Democrats and Republicans announced they had worked out a way to pass legislation that would force a re-examination of the Schiavo case in federal court. This seemed ludicrous. Congress' new approach would be different, however. It would require, a brand-new trial on all of the facts. House Majority Leader Tom DeLay announced at a press conference that not even Democrats would object to this approach. Under Congressional rules, the House would be called back from its "district work period" (a euphemism for "vacation") to vote early Monday morning. That Sunday night included hours of debate on the matter, with a largely Republican cast arguing the pressing need to "save" Ms. Schiavo from "starvation."

Several physicians in Congress, including Senator Bill Frist (R/TN), even appeared to be able to do long-distance diagnostic assessment from 950 miles away, based on watching a snippet of a four-year-old video of her eyes seemingly following the motion of a balloon passing in front of her face. The complete video showed five similar passes without a hint of recognition, suggesting the shorter clip had been released by Ms. Schiavo's parents to create the impression that their daughter was making a conscious decision. Unfortunately, come Monday, the bill passed overwhelmingly.

Shortly after this vote, I obtained a tape recording of DeLay speaking to the Family Research Council. "One thing that God has brought to us is Terri Schiavo, to help elevate the visibility of what is going on in America, attacks against the conservative movement, against me and against many others." He continued that a "whole syndicate" of "do-gooder" forces were arrayed against him in a "huge nationwide concerted effort to destroy everything we believe in."

Senator Bill Frist and Congressman Tom Delay hold emergency session to require federal court review in Schiavo case. Frist "diagnosed" her as possibly able to recover, without examining her. Delay claimed his ethics problems were parallel to her situation. Source: Chip Somodevilla/Getty Images

He was comparing his ethics problems to the fate of Ms. Schiavo. Our communications staff decided it would be good to give this tape exclusively to one journalist and we all decided that David Kirkpatrick of *The New York Times* was the best choice. It was a front-page story for two days and everybody in the news media wanted to get the tape as well. A few critics insisted that we were engaged in the unethical practice of having "spies" observe DeLay. My response was simply that when powerful political figures like DeLay choose to try to meet secretly with Religious Right activists to forge legislation, it affects fundamental rights of all Americans, and the public has a right to know about it.

Eventually, justice was served for both Schiavo and DeLay. Ms. Schiavo was allowed to have the tube removed by action of federal judge Stanley F. Birch, Jr., appointed by George H.W. Bush , who blasted both the President George W. Bush and Congress for ever getting involved in the matter, asserting that both had "acted in a manner demonstrably at odds with our Founding Fathers' blueprint for the governance of a free people, our Constitution." An appeals court upheld that decision, and the Supreme Court would not consider it.

As to DeLay, he received justice too. He threatened to have all the federal judges involved impeached (which never happened). He had been indicted by a Texas grand jury for campaign money laundering and had to leave the role of Majority Leader under Republican caucus rules. Choosing not to seek re-election, he resigned in June 2006. He was convicted of these crimes and sentenced to three years in prison in 2011, but the conviction was later overturned by Texas courts.

Ernest "Jim" Istook (R/OK) represented Oklahoma in the House from 1993 to 2006, and was the lead supporter of efforts to amend the United States Constitution to permit organized prayer in public schools. Opponents of this measure often wore buttons reading "Istook Is Mistook." We had numerous debates on radio and television, but the most noteworthy interchange was in San Antonio, Texas, at the annual convention of social studies teachers at a Sunday morning debate on the merits of his effort, the so-called "Religious Freedom Amendment." The audience response to his proposal was mixed, but it seemed that most of its members were on my side. "Sam" certainly was. He came up after the session and said, "Do you see my broken nose?" The disjointed bones were apparent. He explained how he got it. His Chicago public school teacher, Mrs. Smith, whom he characterized as a woman with "good intentions" who was fearful for his soul as a Jew and wanted him to get to know Jesus, allowed him to leave the classroom when she began praying each morning, but she reminded him repeatedly that while he was sitting outside, his fellow students were praying for him. After school one day, students went a tad beyond praying for him. A dozen of them attacked him and left him with that broken nose.

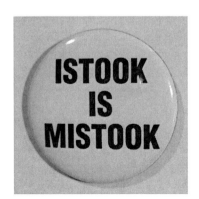

Istook is Mistook button widely distributed during Istook's efforts to pass school prayer amendment.

Congressman Istook and I were both flying out of the San Antonio airport in the early afternoon, and he asked if I'd like to join him for lunch. Of course, I accepted the invitation and learned that he actually had a sense of humor. He began discussing the upcoming crisis with computers when we hit the next millennial. In this Y2K crisis, many people feared computers would not recognize that it was 2000 because they had been programmed with only the last two digits of the year. He asked if I wanted to know what a recent meeting of the Republican caucus had concluded about this: "Most of the caucus decided that if the computers just flip back to 1900, they'd like it better that way," he said. Not a bad joke for a conservative Congressman.

Americans United had put in an enormous effort to defeat Istook's Religious Freedom Amendment effort, which came to a vote on June 4, 1998. Congressman Chet Edwards, a Democrat from Texas and one of the most vocal opponents of the idea, told me before the vote that he feared that the half-million-dollar ad campaign by the Christian Coalition was "costing us votes." As the vote went on, with the electronic tally of green "yeas" and red "nays" appearing on a big screen that alphabetically lists Members, the "nays" finally reached 203. A number of hopelessly undecided Members were voting *against* it, and the vote was sixty-one votes short of the two-thirds necessary to move the amendment to the Senate. We had prevailed. I was happy, of course, but chagrined that a majority of the House had actually voted to repeal part of the Bill of Rights.

Istook did not go away. By September 1999 he was back introducing a similar constitutional amendment and scheduled a big press event that included ten gospel choirs joining him on the west steps of the Capitol. The site had to be changed as storms preceding Hurricane Floyd began hitting Washington and the venue had to be shifted first to a House annex behind the House office buildings and then to the Bible Way Church, ten blocks away. The press was confused by these venue changes but enough showed up to get him some attention. The whole presentation was emceed by Bill Murray, not the comic actor but the son of famous atheist and school prayer foe Madelyn Murray O'Hare. Murray had recently converted to Christianity and wanted to spend his time trying to "restore the damage" his mother had done. Guest speakers included fired New York City schoolteacher Mildred Rosario, who had tried to convert her young pupils to Christianity by having Christian students form prayer circles around the non-converted ones. Thunderous applause came following a New Mexico woman who did a mind-numbing recitation of "Mary Had a Little Lamb," which moved from its traditional nursery rhyme to doggerel poetry as it made a belabored point that the "Lamb of God'' had been barred from school along with Mary's woolly pet. The aforementioned Tom DeLay was present as well and he announced that "no prayer can be uttered in America's schools," a comment that the Religion News Service labeled an "outright lie." That very day an estimated two million students across the country had participated in Rally Round the Pole events where they gathered around the flagpole to pray before classes began. There were 10,000 Bible clubs in high schools, and, of course, millions of young people prayed privately.

Istook himself, who had been a broadcaster before becoming a politician, intoned that an "actual representative of one of the groups that files these lawsuits against prayers" was "right here in this room." He glowered in my direction as the audience booed. I half expected that, following the lead of "Mary's Little Lamb," he might point me out like the Baby Bear, who said about *Goldilocks*, "and she's still here," referring to her presence in the bed. I walked over to Istook as he was leaving and said he should feel free to use my name in future speeches.

Neither the 1999 version nor his subsequent versions in 2001 or 2003 got out of the Judiciary Committee. He eventually ran an unsuccessful campaign to become Oklahoma's governor. He then worked for a bit at the Heritage Foundation, and I ran into him walking to lunch one afternoon. He became a guest on a radio show I was doing, endorsing an idea that the Oklahoma legislature had adopted that I found brilliant. When legislators want to amend an existing law, they must "link" their proposal to a complete description of how it changes current law. Congress should do that too. So, to Mr. Istook, thanks for one good joke and one good idea. Sorry he didn't have more of either.

Chapter 6

THE PRESS, INCLUDING SOME EXTRAORDINARY JOURNALISTS

I have a dim recollection of the television coverage of the coronation of Queen Elizabeth when I was five years old, and slightly more vivid recall of seeing a "news headlines" pamphlet with the headline, "Thing Shot in Nepal Could Be Snowman." Of course, by high school, I was foraging through as much news as possible. Perhaps, I thought, I should become a journalist. As with music, though, I became a person who loved to work with journalists.

I have always enjoyed speaking to the press and appearing on radio and television. I managed to show up on virtually every television and radio show anyone listens to as well as some so small that I felt like only the host and I were hearing or seeing it. There are a few notable exceptions: never been on with Bill Maher and never been interviewed by Amy Goodman. I am disappointed by the latter exclusion but not at all bothered by the former.

When I first got to Washington, the highpoint of my interaction with journalists was speaking with Daniel Schorr from a telephone in a phone booth. This was long before the existence of even the most primitive form of cellphones, which were giant phones in small suitcases that you could plug into your car's cigarette lighter and then carry out and about for approximately two calls before they lost power. Schorr's reporting on Watergate was a centerpiece of the CBS coverage of the Nixon scandal—and got him on Nixon's notorious "enemies list." The mere thought that he wanted to get some information from me (statistics about the desertion rate in the military, as I recall) was a fabulous opportunity. I was an unquoted source, but I had spoken to a journalistic giant.

My very first television appearance was on a local Fox affiliate newscast the day President Gerald Ford announced his ill-fated "clemency program" for Vietnam War resisters. Washington's local

Channel Five News filmed me making a call to a military deserter's wife in Toronto to find out if her Green Beret husband would be coming home to do his alternative service. The only voice they used was hers. She defiantly said no one in the resistance community would even consider returning under the conditions Ford had laid out.

A few weeks later, I was on a show with Congressman John Conyers (D/MI) hosted by a local Presbyterian minister and aired early Sunday mornings. Stations showed their limited commitment to following the Federal Communications Commission's regulations to broadcast public affairs programs by scheduling them at such low-listener times. Still, some people saw that program and called me.

These early encounters gave me a sense of the power of media, particularly television. It is hard for people today to imagine the extraordinary excitement of being on television in those pre-cable network days. It didn't get you the celebrity of Paris Hilton or the notoriety of Abbie Hoffman, but it marked you as doing something most people had not. There is a well-done movie with Nicole Kidman called *To Die For*, in which a New Hampshire teacher has an affair with one of her students. Her trial is widely covered by the media, and she says, "If you aren't on television, you are nobody."

What follows is a sample of my interactions with some very talented women and men–and a few substantially less worthy ones.

The Big Names in Syndication or Cable

The syndicated *Phil Donahue Show* was one of the greatest achievements in daytime television. Phil exposed America, and, in particular, American homemakers, to a world they might not have experienced otherwise. He brought Madalyn Murray O'Hare, the country's best-known atheist in the Fifties and Sixties into homes on numerous occasions, saying to CNN after his retirement that "Madalyn was the only person I had on by herself on more than one occasion." He made America aware of gay men and lesbians, bisexuals and crossdressers, the whole panoply of human sexual diversity. He did it wisely and without unnecessary shock to those who had not seen any representatives of these communities.

When Phil Donahue's staff called my office to see if I would come on his show to discuss the possible return of the military draft, as I described in Book 1, it was a very big deal.

When I started work at the American Civil Liberties Union, I appeared a second time on Phil's show to discuss religious liberty conflicts. When I was introduced by Phil, he said "I never leave the house anymore without an ACLU lawyer." My third shot was near the end of his television career when his previously overflowing studio audience was not as easy to acquire. This program was also about the Religious Right and featured a long-distance appearance by Senator Arlen Specter of Pennsylvania, one of the last Republican moderates in the Senate, with the head of the New York State affiliate of the American Family Association.

On that show, the smaller audience didn't seem terribly enthusiastic. Phil stopped the taping and said, "I know some of you were hoping we would have 'men in kilts' on the show, but we don't, and it would be great if you had some questions for our guests." The audience came through. Phil had the practice of going to the Green Room after shows and thanking each guest personally. The guest from the American Family Association was so insulting and belligerent that I was almost as embarrassed for him as I was for Phil. As always, Phil kept his cool but clearly had not expected the guy's ranting about abortion, religion, and "unfairness" in the media.

When Phil's syndicated show came to an end, he hosted a debate show on a new cable network where he was paired with Russian journalist Vladimir Pozner for an hour each weeknight. I used to do that show quite frequently and occasionally would brief Phil on issues he was discussing that night even when I was not a guest. On one occasion, I talked with him while driving over the Golden Gate Bridge, AU's great development director Marjorie Spitz Nagrotsky held the cellphone so I could drive safely. Phil never hid his beliefs, but he was incredibly respectful of people with whom he disagreed. He kindly gave a plug to Americans United for Separation of Church and State during an interview in *Entertainment Weekly*. He also wrote a highly successful fundraising letter for Americans United. The only media personality I knew who had as much enthusiastic interest in exploring issues as Walter Cronkite and Phil Donohue was Al Franken, during his brief tenure on the radio network Air America. He would occasionally call up a guest he was going to speak with the next day and spend an hour on the phone to make sure he was aware of the nuances of the topic. Al took that same mindset to the Senate where he was generally the most prepared questioner on the Senate Judiciary Committee, until accusations of sexual harassment regrettably and unfairly cut short his Senate career.

Oprah Winfrey began doing her syndicated television show after Phil's was well underway. I only did that show once and was unimpressed with her "journalism." My participation in Oprah's program came right after the Ed Meese Pornography Commission wrapped up its work.

What bothered me about that show was that Oprah allowed an Alliance Defending Freedom staff member to sit in the audience and ask a question without anyone indicating that he was with that conservative Christian legal advocacy group. Phil would never have done that. I considered Oprah's conduct "junk journalism," putting on a show. I never watched her show again. Possibly worse, Oprah hosted two insufferable characters on her show—Dr. Phil McGraw and Dr. Mehmet Oz, both of whom went on the create their own useless or worse media empires. When Oz ran for the Senate in 2022, she endorsed his opponent and Oz's opponent, John Fetterman, won.

When Oprah was campaigning for Barack Obama, she occasionally held fundraisers at her Chicago mansion. A well-respected constitutional scholar and CEO of CHILD USA, an interdisciplinary think tank to prevent child abuse and neglect, told me that Oprah stood up as the event began and told the crowd this was her house, and she wouldn't be chatting with any of them.

Phil and Oprah were the most watched daytime talk show hosts in television history, but they had some competition from the likes of Geraldo Rivera, Jerry Springer, and Sally Jessy Raphael (noted for her bright red framed glasses). I had one Geraldo experience (also about the Porn Commission).

My panel consisted of a man who was proud to say he spent a great deal of time with prostitutes, a major adult film actress of that era, Gloria Leonard, and a few anti-pornography activists. The one exchange I remember most clearly was when an audience member said she had been horrified when her teenage daughter received an unsolicited Victoria's Secret catalogue in the mail and Gloria noted, "How do you know she hadn't ordered it herself?" The audience members didn't take well to the remark and there were scattered boos throughout the theater.

I always liked Gloria. She once called my house, and when my son answered, she gave him her phone number and said, "I worked with your father on censorship, and I'd like to talk to him about a different issue." When I returned her call, she said she had been replaced as editor of *High Society* magazine by a younger woman and wondered if she had any right to claim age discrimination under federal law. She did have, but I felt awkward asking her how old she was to see if she qualified to establish that eligibility. Since in most cases the Act protects those forty or older, Gloria was well protected.

Mainstream and Polarizing Press

I always enjoyed my occasional appearances with Anderson Cooper, but my absolute favorite time was being on with him to debate anti-evolutionist Ken Ham, the man who created both the Creation Museum in Tennessee and the life-size replica of Noah's Ark in the middle of a water park called Ark Encounter. The ostensible purpose of this debate was to discuss my claim that Ham was unconstitutionally seeking taxpayer support for his Ark Park through a combination of construction projects that would benefit this attraction and certain loans. Discussing tax policies is usually dull television. In preparation for this one, I did a deep dive into Ham's website, which provided ammunition of a more engaging kind.

The third guest that evening was Jeffrey Toobin, CNN's chief legal analyst. He was non-committal on the legal theory of my argument, noting that Tennessee would be prohibited from funding this project only if it was a clearly religious entity like a church or church school. Since at the time, Ark Encounter was labeling itself a "ministry" of the church, Answers In Genesis, I figured we could make that case.

More interesting than the funding Ham sought from the government was my claim that Tennessee shouldn't, as a matter of educational policy, fund junk science and mislead the students of the state. My evidence? Ham planned to populate his ark with humans, animals, *and dinosaurs*. Somewhat incredulous, Anderson Cooper asked Ham to address my assertion. Ham said: "Well of course all these were on the ark because the Earth is only 6000 years old." This age of Earth argument is routinely made by creationists, but even the Reverend Pat Robertson later criticized Ham for using it because it, "Makes Christians look foolish." I continued my biological critique with the observation, "And the ark will also contain unicorns." Anderson again wanted Ham's response, which was a bit more muted, but I noted that that very afternoon, this claim was on his website and said, "I'd like to think that people realize that unicorns are *fictional* animals."

After the segment was over, I went out into the Green Room at CNN in Washington and met one of Cooper's producers. She said: "Barry, you know you have crushed the dreams of thousands of little girls," who like my own daughter, and now my twin granddaughters, Evangelina and Victoria, have a special place in their hearts for unicorns.

Big Names in Radio and Television

Bill Press had been the chair of the California Democratic Party from 1993-1996 but had moved to Washington. A prolific writer and columnist, he also became the co-host with Pat Buchanan of the best version of CNN's *Crossfire*. The hosts that followed were Paul Begala and Tucker Carlson. Press and Buchanan regrouped for a similar program on MSNBC, appropriately named *Buchanan & Press*. This show was canceled about a year later because both hosts opposed United States involvement in the Iraq War of 2003.

Press eventually left cable television but continued to do a syndicated radio show and got a White House press pass during the Obama administration. Wherever Bill was broadcasting, he had me on as a frequent guest to talk about civil liberties, religion, and politics.

On that final radio show, he operated from a small studio in a building just off Capitol Hill. I regret that his show was literally the only program where I was once late for an appearance. Bedeviled by construction, an accident, and somewhat unfamiliar roads, I missed the first ten minutes of my scheduled shot, getting wrong information about where to park from one of his producers. Slightly out of breath, I managed to make a few points and the show wrapped up. Bill wasn't upset but gave me a piece of great advice: "Use the app WAZE because it has more up-to-date traffic tracking. It's the new app that takes into account actual traffic snafus and routes you around them." I downloaded it immediately and was never late for anything again.

Bill also moderated a discussion on activism with feminist icon Eleanor Smeal and me one night. He is a fine moderator and knows just when to interject his thoughts into the conversation. He stunned the crowd by noting that "the invention of cable television was the worst thing that ever happened to the intelligence of the American people." Not only was he accurate then, but he was even more prescient as we entered the era of Donald Trump. I would occasionally fill in as host of Bill's show, including one Friday when one of my guests was a plastic talking action figure of Ann Coulter.

Thom Hartmann was a progressive talk show host long before the liberal network Air America was a glint in anyone's eyes. He doggedly pursued placements on individual radio stations around the country, while writing a dozen books. I loved being on his shows, including his early afternoon television feed on Facebook and his televised daily show on the RT network. This initially stood for Russia Today, which became too controversial a name, so it rebranded solely with its initials. Hartmann occasionally did shows that focused on "most brilliant minds" and I was honored to be placed in that category when my book *God and Government* came out, a compendium of my writings and speeches with new "connective tissue" to tie issues together and update incidents in those earlier communications.

What I admired most about Thom is that he knew so much about so many issues that he could have thoughtful insights to offer to his "expert" guests. After one particularly damaging Supreme Court decision that allowed a church-related school to become eligible for a state program in Missouri to donate shredded automobile tires to school playgrounds, a seemingly trivial financial contribution which metastasized into more government funding for religious schools, we discussed why this was unconstitutional. Then Thom raised a different non-legal question I had never even considered: Could It be dangerous to have children play on tire bits that were oil-based and might contain cancer-causing chemicals? Upon doing post-show research on this question myself, it turned out that there is scientific evidence to back up this possibility. Who knew? Thom Hartmann. Indeed a 2012 study of tire mulch in Spain found that all samples in playgrounds contained at least one hazardous chemical, and many contained high concentrations of several. A later study at Yale University found that, unlike woodchips, fewer than a third of playgrounds using tires met standards for "head impact safety" while all using woodchips did.

Ed Schultz worked for Dial Global. I always enjoyed doing Ed's radio and television shows. He had been recruited from his radio perch in North Dakota by Tom Athans, then husband of Senator Debbie Stabenow of Michigan, to become the counterweight to Rush Limbaugh. I had dinner with Tom and Senator Stabenow at a Triangle Foundation dinner in Michigan. Ed had met with big Democratic Party donors in Washington and his syndicated radio show was launched, eventually getting to more than 100 stations and to Sirius/XM satellite radio. His progressive viewpoint was one of the few commercial efforts at creating a non-conservative voice on talk radio.

By this time, Air America had collapsed from the utter incompetence of its new management. If for no other reason than to achieve a quasi-balance on some local radio stations, Ed found more airspace than even he had expected. MSNBC was on the lookout for a show in the late afternoons and Ed was hired. Then Ed Schultz was fired by MSNBC for being principled in his opposition to the Pacific Pipeline, an issue never discussed by most other alleged liberals on the network. He took on hosting an evening show on RT. Schultz said in an interview that he had prepared a piece for MSNBC about Senator Bernie Sanders' presidential candidate announcement but was told by the network President that "You're not covering Bernie Sanders." When his negative view on the Pacific Pipeline emerged along with his support for the Presidential candidacy of Senator Bernie Sanders, the network dumped him, profiting as it did from the revenues of big oil companies and its close association with the Clintons.

I was often on his television shows on Fridays to discuss whatever outrages the Religious Right had engaged in over the past week and was often paired with Lizz Winstead (one of the founders of Air America who was herself deposed from that network) or John Fuegelsang. Every year when the Christian Coalition or the Family Research Council held their yearly conferences (hatefests), I would report in on what had happened there. I was disappointed when Ed was fired, but once he took on an evening spot on RT network, we would chat about religious conservatives and rightwing political activities. I never got the impression that Ed was required to toe some Russian Party Line on foreign affairs. He once said he felt that he had more journalistic integrity on RT than at MSNBC. Some colleagues at Americans United urged me not to appear on the RT network, but if I was willing to show up on Fox News, I didn't think showing up on a possibly communist network could do me any damage.

Fox News and People Who Should Have Been on Fox

During his heyday, I spent many evenings with Bill O'Reilly, who, in one segment, referred to me both as "one of my favorite guests" and "a loon." These are not mutually exclusive categories, but it takes a little juggling to get the connection. The strangest single appearance on his show also related to creationism. He claimed that God must have been the literal creator because the world is basically good and it works. The alternative, random selection, was bad. I tried to explain that randomness is not some inherently evil operation of the universe. It is simply a description of events. Obviously, the evidence that there were plenty of species that died out made it clear that not everything in the universe succeeded. O'Reilly would have none of that.

Most progressives would never go on his show because he was so argumentative and/or too stupid to have a discussion with. But I often just wanted to try out arguments with him as a test for going on more serious programs later that evening or the next morning. It was, however, easy for me to believe the worst of him when he was caught up in sex scandals and fired from Fox, because his arrogance alone would fit in perfectly with his inability to ever believe his "word" would be challenged.

In another appearance he said: "Today, I am going to turn you around, bring you over to my side once and for all." To this I responded: "Give it your best shot." We spent the next five or six minutes discussing President George W. Bush's use of overtly religious language in his speeches. O'Reilly felt that Bush's references to religion were no different than similar language used by Presidents Jefferson and Madison, as if their occasional references to a deity were comparable to Bush's obvious efforts to appeal to evangelical conservatives. Bush had recently made a reference to the "Great Commission," which is the charge to bring the Christian gospel to all the world. He had also quoted an old Baptist hymn in his State of the Union address, "Power, wonder-working power." In its full version, the hymn concludes "in the precious blood of the Lamb." This is a kind of code for evangelicals, whose post-State of the Union commenters celebrated it the next day.

Bush could get even more explicit, telling journalist Bob Woodward that when he makes decisions on military matters, he uses "God-given values" not "United States-created values." The President also announced that he would only nominate federal judges who "know our rights come from God." This is the kind of rhetoric that causes some of Bush's supporters to believe that God chose Bush to be president. According to Tim Goeglein, a high-level White House staffer, "I think President Bush is God's man at this hour, and I say this with a great deal of humility." This obviously leads to the conclusion that Bush's will and God's will are identical and that to criticize Bush is to critique God.

Bush was also good at saying things like "government cannot put hope in people's hearts." Really? Ask the high school student next door how she feels when the the government notifies her a Pell grant will help fund college. Ask a person whose home is destroyed in a hurricane if federal disaster relief provides a sense of hope. Talk to an impoverished family who eats because they get food stamps. *Of course*, government can provide hope. Despite Bush's talk of religion and values, his administration chose not to.

At about this time, *The Boston Globe* ran a sad story about the U.S. Department of Veterans Affairs telling a large homeless shelter in Northampton, Massachusetts that it would lose funding for about half of its beds. Why? Apparently "faith-based" shelters had been getting a leg up on other providers by checking a box on their grant applications indicating that they were "faith-based." A leader of Veterans United which had run the homeless shelter that was losing so much funding objected that secular shelters with proven records of success were losing support. As one advocate for the homeless put it, "This means more people will be sleeping on the streets and more people will die." Facts like these were unpersuasive to O'Reilly.

After John Kasich (R/OH) lost his seat in Congress, he was given a talk show on Saturday nights on Fox News. He was not much of an interviewer as he babbled on about issues that he knew very little about. Nevertheless, he was always interested in discussing issues of religion and the law. His producers called constantly to get a guest from Americans United on with him. It got to the point where my colleague Rob Boston and I had to draw straws to see who would have to waste Saturday night speaking with him.

As noted, he seemed to be so enamored by his own voice that he barely listened. One night he rambled past the ending time of his program and, as I watched the in-studio clock move past the hour, I really couldn't believe that he was so clueless that he didn't see the clock. He drifted into the Geraldo Rivera time slot, something I suspect ticked off Geraldo. Paying attention to the time is "talk show hosting 101." I did find a way to keep him quiet though. I would just say "Congressman," which apparently flipped him back to the time when he had actual clout (during his nine terms in the House) and he would immediately stop talking, as if savoring the glow of his past job.

Kasich went on to be the governor of Ohio and was later hired by CNN to present the moderate-Republican-critical-of-Trump view. Kasich is not now, nor was he ever, a moderate on the issues that matter.

Tucker Carlson wrote in his first autobiography that he decided early in his tenure in Washington as a journalist for The Weekly Standard that you got famous here if you were on television. He describes how excited he was to be invited on a cable show with former Secretary of the Army Clifford Alexander to discuss a military topic he knew nothing about. Even in the days of slightly longer segments than we see today, he was good at faking knowledge and in fact was noticed by bookers for other shows as "that nice looking guy who wears bowties."

Carlson was one of the few pundits let go by three networks: PBS, CNN, and MSNBC. He was also the first contestant voted off the 2006 season of *Dancing with the Stars* for his less-than-sparkling Cha-Cha dance with Elena Grinenko. A judge pointed out that he spent too much time sitting in a chair. I was a guest on his shows on CNN and MSNBC and found him mildly amusing. Nevertheless, he ended up with a primetime show on Fox News, after proving himself by being a guest or guest host there. Certainly, Fox is where he belonged all along.

On one *Crossfire* episode, we were debating the posting of the Ten Commandments on government buildings. Carlson asked if I wanted to blast the image of Moses from the Supreme Court display of famous lawgivers in a frieze that surrounds the chamber. I asked him if he could read what was on the tablets and he joked, "Not without my contacts."

"You couldn't even read it with them in—there are only two words visible and they are in Hebrew. So, unlike the Commandments posters we are discussing here written in English in big letters, nobody would even know what the Supreme Court depiction even is, much less what it says."

My favorite Carlson moment did not occur on television. He was the first speaker at a rightwing religious conference put on by huckster Ralph Reed. Carlson came out wearing jeans, joshing that this "is what I wear when I'm not on the air." I was sitting in the front row so I could tape some of the later speakers and he noticed me. "Wow, Barry Lynn is here." People began applauding, so he quickly added, "No, I didn't mean you should applaud. He disagrees with everything we stand for."

Tucker has unfortunately gone from his amusing phase into a worse space, perhaps culminating in his July 2020 comments on his daily Fox News primetime show where he said that decorated double amputee Senator Tammy Duckworth hates America and is a moron. Carlson can always rely on gold sales and the insufferable Mike Lindell My Pillow ads to sustain some income for the network. It is sometimes hard to take his "common man" act given his Yale education and family wealth from the Swanson Company of TV dinner fame.

By the 2005 Presidential campaign almost all of television had become a cesspool of ignorance, further tainted by an utter unwillingness or inability to put anything into historical perspective. It was not just that Fox News was obviously rightwing, but also that the few somewhat moderate people on the network were relegated to covering issues of limited significance. Greta Van Susteren had been a clever co-anchor of CNN's midday legal affairs show *Burden of Proof*, but now she was doing an hour-long crime show, talking to people who often had no actual connection to the cases she was covering. They simply bloviated about what their past status (e.g., former prosecutor, former police detective) led them to think about the current topic.

Even worse was Nancy Grace, formerly of *CourtTV*, who began to sit in for Larry King. On those shows, she too tended to discuss the same crimes and would even give airtime to "psychic detectives," as if these jerks should be taken seriously for their views, telepathic or otherwise. MSNBC had created an evening show for former Republican Florida Congressman Joe Scarborough. The boring Scarborough literally took most of the format of *The O'Reilly Factor* and placed his head and voice in place of Bill O'Reilly's. Scarborough was so insecure about his ability to have an argument with anyone on the left (a well-deserved fear) that he would often have himself and up to three other conservatives to do battle with a single liberal. The liberal would often spend his or her first soundbite complaining about, or at least pointing out the disparity in voices, thus confirming for Joe's small cadre of conservative viewers that leftists really didn't have anything of substance to contribute in the first place. I was occasionally that lone liberal, but I never complained about the format.

Scarborough also cut off the microphone to make sure he always got "the last word;" O'Reilly rarely did that. He simply spoke over you as you were giving what he proffered to you as "the final word."

Really Smart Conservatives

Of all the conservative women I debated, none was as smart or as pleasant as Janet Parshall who did a daily radio show for the Salem Radio network and later for Moody Radio. For years she and her husband Craig, who was the general counsel for the National Religious Broadcasters group, hosted me. Despite being married to Craig, she was remarkably fair in moderating our debates. We generally spent a full hour on a single topic and took plenty of listener phone calls. It was unheard of to spend an entire hour looking at both sides of contentious issues like court challenges to the Pledge of Allegiance, National Day of Prayer, and the clash of asserted rights between the LGBTQ+ community and Christian conservatives who don't want to serve that community by baking cakes or photographing same sex weddings.

This format also gave Craig and me a chance to discuss "first principles," the philosophical underpinnings of our views of the Constitution. I recall him saying once, "There has to be a healthy breathing space between church and state" but accusing me of wanting to "hermetically seal off" the two. I told him that I prefer to think about this as keeping a "decent distance" between those entities—similar to the way chaperones at high school dances used to keep tabs on the distance between slow dancing couples. He also said that it is wrong for the government to "control the levers" of religion. I was having some plumbing done at our house at this time, so I moved quickly to a plumbing analogy: "I believe government has the right and the responsibility to control the levers that regulate any water flow that could flood the neighborhood, but it shouldn't regulate every spiritual spigot that only has a small leak."

Who won these debates? I'm sure only the National Security Council knows for sure. One afternoon we discussed whether Congress had the right to ask mega-ministry leaders like Benny Hinn and Bishop Eddie Long to voluntarily provide financial information that could explain their very high salaries, Pacific Ocean overlook parsonages, and expensive private aircraft. Every single caller supported my view that this was entirely appropriate and rejected Craig's "hands off" the ministries approach. That was the only issue where I had that level of success with my side of the argument.

Janet also arranged several debates at the big National Religious Broadcasters Convention, usually held in Nashville. They were well attended and included respectful interchanges on hot church/state topics.

When someone tells you, "You ought to do his radio show" (as in, somebody else's show), it is occasionally a good idea to pay attention. Pat Buchanan left his syndicated radio program *Pat Buchanan and Company.* By that time, I was the only "company" he had left—Bob Beckel, Juan Williams, Chris Matthews, and Ben Wattenberg having long abandoned the company car. He told me that Lt. Col. Oliver North was starting a new radio program and I ought to go and do it. I was non-committal but eventually decided to try it just once.

I had not met North, but the American Civil Liberties Union had come to his defense during some of his legal proceedings because we thought that Congressional investigations of the so-called Iran-Contra affair had so sullied the waters that an actual trial was tainted, since the hearings violated North's Fifth Amendment right against self-incrimination. The Iran-Contra matter involved serious allegations that North had sold weapons to Iran and then sent the proceeds to rebel forces in Nicaragua. However, if potential jurors had watched any of the extensive hearings on this topic, could they reasonably be expected to ignore what they heard there and deliberate solely on what was heard at the trial for which they were sitting? We were skeptical, and there was a substantial amount of showboating, including an insulting reference to North's "costume" which was his Naval dress uniform, by Democratic Congresspeople.

On my first guest appearance on the new North show, I had a good time and was surprised by how gracious he was and how non-belligerent he seemed. Frankly, I did think I had mopped up the floor with his ridiculous arguments about the First Amendment. I had a brief chat with him after the show in which he asked me to consider becoming a regular co-host for an hour each week. Why not? I accepted the invitation and continued in that role, usually on air for the last of his three hours on Friday afternoon, for close to four years. North told me after the first year or so that that hour was the most highly rated hour of his week on syndicated networks around the country. I could believe that.

Lynn revels as thorn in side of religious conservatives

Separationist calls on theological training in the cause

By Julia Duin
THE WASHINGTON TIMES

Just the other day a genuine political "Odd Couple" was holding forth on radio. Oliver North, the star of the 1987 Iran-Contra hearings and today a businessman and radio talk-show host, was going head to head with the Rev. Barry Lynn, executive director of Americans United for Separation of Church and State.

The conversation was about Gov. George W. Bush's celebrated description of New York Times reporter Adam Clymer.

"It's not a sin to call a guy an anatomical part," Mr. North said. One reason why Bush has a 20-point lead among men is that he's a man."

"Using the 'a-hole' word is being a man?" Mr. Lynn asked.

Photos by Ross D. Franklin/The Washington Times

Barry Lynn, of Americans United for Separation of Church and State, is a frequent radio and TV "talking head" on religion-related issues.

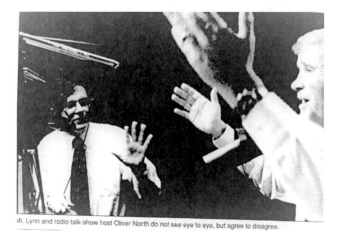

Mr. Lynn and radio talk-show host Oliver North do not see eye to eye, but agree to disagree.

Lynn and Lt. Col. Oliver North do their weekly radio show. Source: **The Washington Times.**

I particularly remember a few broadcasts in which we pulled off the equivalent of Orson Welles' spoof, *War of the Worlds*. On the day that the federal government began implementation of the "no call list" (in theory, salespeople could not call to sell you anything if you were on a list of people who didn't want such calls), there was a massive influx of ticked off consumers calling who didn't want to be bothered by these phone solicitations. North and I started that show by discussing some Supreme Court case but were then (as planned) interrupted by his producer, Griff Jenkins (who went on to be a Fox News Network correspondent). "Guys, we were just contacted by the White House and they would like to have all radio talk show hosts take phone inquiries about being placed on the 'no call' list because the government switchboards are overwhelmed." We noted that we'd be happy to do this and found that the claim of blocked switchboards was so plausible that our phone intake system was quickly overwhelmed with every line lit. That's when the fun began.

I am convinced that all the people who called in believed we were turning their information over to some government agency and that they would not be bothered by roofers, lawn servicers, mortgage companies, and similar entities. We had decided in advance that we would alternate answering the calls. I went first and was told by a woman that she wanted to get on the "do not call" list because she was not in need of the stuff they were selling. I asked her: "Could I just ask you how much you weigh?" North of course interjected, "You can't ask somebody that." "Ollie, I just want to make sure that she does not want to get any calls. If she thinks she has a weight problem, maybe she'd like to have a footnote in her record that says—'willing to be called by weight loss programs.'" It went on like this for the entire hour, with every line still lit when we signed off. Since the actual "do not call" list has not been particularly effective in stopping unwanted solicitations, it is possible that the people we talked to were no worse off than if they had reached the official office that afternoon.

During a trip Joanne and I took to Australia, we had arranged to have me call in to North's show. After some difficulty getting the time difference figured out, I called and reported that I had learned that Australia has the largest number of species of deadly snakes, insects, and even plants of anywhere on earth. North asked if I had seen any of them, and when I responded that I had not yet, he responded, "Could you stay for another week?"

Some of the things that happened around this show were most interesting. After one show, we were leaving and about to get on the elevator and a young woman arrived to get on at the same time. When North said, "You first," she replied, "No" with one of the most withering stares of distaste I have ever seen.

One day when North had been hired to do a nightly show with Paul Begala on MSNBC, I was over at their studio to do some other show and he said, "They want me to do a 'hit' (television jargon for a interview) in a few minutes. Could you just start the show?" So, I did and decided to announce that North had been fired and that I would now be the sole host of his former show. I went right to the phones. Astonishing as it was to me, the first two callers (again, believing everything they heard) said they were glad I was going to be on alone. One said, "You seem to be more open-minded"; the other said something about North being "arrogant." After forty-five minutes, North came into the studio and pretended to be outraged and then claimed he was going to tie me up and put duct tape over my mouth. I mumbled authentically.

We also had a good time with "contests," a talk radio staple. I offered prizes from my "back of the closet tie collection." We once held a history contest based on a test that had been recently highlighted in the *New York Times*. Ostensibly, this was to see whether my supporters (people who had gone to public schools) or his (private school attendees) would be better at answering questions. One question was the reason for the acquisition of land now constituting New Mexico, Utah, Nevada, Arizona, California, Texas, parts of Colorado, and Kansas. The options for answers included The War with Mexico, the Louisiana Purchase, and the Gadsden Purchase. When a caller answered, "Gadsden Purchase" (a wrong answer), I probed: "Are you sure?" He said "Yes." Then I started humming a few bars of the ditty "The Mexican Hat Dance" and repeated my inquiry about sticking with his answer, followed by a direct question whether there were any Mexican restaurants where he lived. He just never took the hint that The War with Mexico was the correct answer. After that contest we both agreed that America needed a better education system.

North is still a highly controversial figure, no less so because he became the Board President of the National Rifle Association. North was fired from that position after a squabble with its longtime director, Wayne LaPierre, amidst accusations that Wayne spent too much money on himself and gave out sweetheart contracts to friends. I hate the NRA, but I can speak reasonably well of North because of some of the policy positions he has and the alacrity with which he moves them forward. For example, I hate the death penalty and found that he does too. At the time we were doing the show together, he was the third most popular fundraiser for the Republican Party and any Republican would be happy to take his phone call. On several occasions when an execution was imminent in a state with a conservative Republican governor, I tracked North down to get him to call that Governor urging clemency for the soon to be executed person. He would do it, but it was not clear that he altered any state executive's decision. The fact that he was making the calls, though, was enough to make me feel good about his commitment to a principle we shared.

I recently found a copy of his first novel inscribed to me as, "My favorite co-host." North told me I would be a character in the third of his novels, but he is now on his fourth book and I don't believe I've shown up yet.

Radio Giants

I really appreciated Michael Robin Jackson from KABC in Los Angeles. He would have a person like me following a proposed piece of legislation on his show every day that a bill was working its way to a resolution in Congress. He'd call and chat about the arcane steps for a proposal, assuming that certain items—bringing back the draft or regulating pornography or flag burning—were interesting enough that people should want to know the steps to passage or defeat that they were going through. He was brilliant. He didn't use his British accent to disguise when he didn't know something, in contrast to Piers Morgan who relies on his accent to cover his lack of knowledge. After moving from South Africa, he became a disc jockey at KHJ where he played Top 40 music, which he reportedly hated. As he phased out of music and into talk, he chatted with callers at a small San Francisco station where comedian Mort Sahl called him the "All Night Psychiatrist," because he tried to solve listeners' problems. After winning critical acclaim, he started an interview show on KABC which lasted for three decades.

I usually did Jackson's show from Washington, but on one trip to Los Angeles to raise money and give a few speeches, I asked if I could come chat in his studio, and he graciously agreed. After about an hour, as I was leaving, he said, "See these two phone banks? This one is from callers in the Los Angeles area. The other one is from callers everywhere else. I only take calls from the first bank." Somehow, it didn't come across as sanctimonious snobbery, just a statement of the truth that an LA caller was more likely to have something useful to say than a caller from Idaho. I couldn't argue with that conclusion once I started hosting call-in shows myself. Jackson died at eighty-seven in 2022.

Diane Rehm was a mainstay on National Public Radio for decades, airing her program from WAMU-FM, the affiliate in Washington DC, and broadcasting from the campus of American University. She was always prepared, willing to air all sides of disputes even if she had (and even had expressed) strong views on the matter, and had marvelous producers who could mix and match guests for incredibly interesting panel discussions. Over the years I was able to express my views on many church and state issues including the Pentacle Quest, church politicking, and whether Muslim women should be permitted to wear veils for their official driver's license photographs. On this last issue, wouldn't it be easier for a police officer stopping a woman failing to stop at a stop sign to find similarities between a veiled driver and a veiled photo on her drivers' license?

My favorite appearance on her show featured response to the horrendous Supreme Court decision in the case of the Hobby Lobby company refusing to cover most effective forms of birth control in their employees' health insurance plans. Hobby Lobby argued that their Board of Directors had a religious objection to covering forms of birth control because they effectively induced abortion, so were "abortifacients."

The panel consisted of Sandra Fluke, who had challenged the decision of her law school to deny similar benefits based on claimed "religious" objections; Julie Rovner, a superb writer for the respected Kaiser Health News; a lawyer for Hobby Lobby; and me. The lawyer was the only one supporting the Court's allowing the company to deny coverage. I have often been the only one to advocate for a position, and it is difficult, but he did a terrible job of rebutting the medical evidence. The medical evidence showed that IUDs and other methods the company wouldn't cover do not cause abortion.

I pointed out Hobby Lobby's hypocrisies. For example, Hobby Lobby allowed employees to invest in the pharmaceutical companies that made the drugs and bought huge amounts of their products from China, which officially permitted its citizens to have only one child, mandating abortion for pregnancies after that first birth. Usually, Diane's guests would hang out for a while and chat after a show, but the Hobby Lobby lawyer couldn't leave the building quickly enough.

Diane left radio when her spasmodic dysphonia became too severe. This condition causes involuntary spasms in the muscles of the voice box which creates all manner of difficulty speaking. During the last few shows I did with her, she had pre-recorded some segments, including the introduction of her guests, but she never lost the ability to ask extraordinary questions. She now does a weekly podcast and continues to promote medical aid in dying, in large part because of the suffering her husband John endured while dying from Parkinson's disease. He refused to eat or drink but received no physician assistance in terminating his suffering.

Mighty Chaos

The grandfather of all cable shoutfests was, of course, *Crossfire*, the CNN show that had started with Pat Buchanan and Tom Braden. In my time, its seat occupants were usually Paul Begala (who is a very smart and serious former advisor to Bill Clinton) and Tucker Carlson (a genuine dimwit who wrote briefly for *National Review*). In late 2004, Comedy Central's Jon Stewart appeared on *Crossfire*, ostensibly to promote his newly published satirical political science textbook. Instead, Stewart lambasted the pair for turning serious news into a joke. Stewart noted that he was himself a comedian and comedians are supposed to do that, but Americans deserved more from people who were supposed to be serious analysts of major issues. His comments were tsunamic. He had dared to say that cable news was squandering its opportunities and trashing thoughtful discourse. CNN bravely defended the show briefly, but then, in early 2005, announced that it was being taken off the air. In what I knew would be my final appearance on the show, I brought a stuffed animal onto the set, just my small way of saying: "Jon Stewart was right. Let's all just get a laugh out of it."

In this polarized time, few programs deliberately tried to have hosts with different viewpoints, except to go at one another, as *Crossfire* did. Ron Reagan and Monica Crowley were exceptions. This pair had a daily show on MSNBC every morning, and they were quite good at it. Obviously, Reagan saw things my way. Indeed, he went on to record a number of powerful commercials with the atheist/separation of church and state group the Freedom from Religion Foundation. Ron and Monica often had two guests and spent an astonishing two segments of an hour on the same topic. This was almost unheard of in that era and is now completely off the table as a format.

My favorite appearance there was with Franklin Graham to discuss his group Samaritan's Purse, which was getting federal funds for disaster relief. Graham insisted that he had the right to use some of his taxpayer funding to distribute stuffed teddy bears with Bible verses on their bellies. Government-funded proselytizing, even with stuffed animals, is not something the Constitution should permit, and I said so. This was the last time Graham agreed to be on with me or with any of the people who worked with me at Americans United.

Outstanding Print Journalists

One Sunday in 2008, I felt like the President. As I looked at the crowd in front of me, Helen Thomas was sitting in the front row, just as she did for decades at the White House briefing room, where she was regularly the first person to be called on at Presidential press conferences as the lead correspondent for United Press International. This was not the White House, though, but a meeting room at St. John's Episcopal Church across from the White House, often dubbed "the Church of the Presidents." (During the COVID-19 pandemic, it was also where President Trump tried to appear religious by holding a Bible upside down while speaking about "riots" that occurred following the death of George Floyd.) Helen had asked me to speak to a group of congregants about the amount of religion in the 2008 election cycle.

Many journalists aided and abetted the inclusion of religion in the political debate that year by asking candidates what they pray for, what their greatest sin was, and what their favorite Bible verse was.

This is not the stuff about which voters should make their electoral decisions. They can do so, just like they can decide based on shoe size or favorite color, but they shouldn't.

Helen took Joanne and me to lunch later in the day and reminded us of the first press encounter she had with George W. Bush the week before he was sworn in. The junior Bush had an informal gathering in the pressroom at the White House and was asked many questions about cabinet appointments and other administrative matters. Helen had a different agenda; she wanted to know why Bush seemed to have so little respect for the separation of church and state. He fumbled around and made some vague response. One of his communications staff called Helen afterward to moan about her "ambush" of the President-elect. That was Helen—cut to the core, ask straightforward questions, and expect clear and honest answers. She knew that if you spend a lot of time "theologizing" during a campaign, you'll be hard pressed to stop once you are in office.

Helen Thomas was fired a few years later for allegedly being too pro-Palestinian in some of her reporting on the Middle East. America lost a genuine truth seeker when that occurred.

United Press International had also been the home of social issues writer David E. Anderson. His beat was anything controversial that had a movement behind it. He was my first close journalist friend in Washington and, indeed, the only journalist I ever got drunk with, which also led to my decision to virtually stop drinking alcohol altogether. In 1974, he had written an article which appeared on the front page of my hometown newspaper, *The Bethlehem Globe Times,* in which I was quoted. It was the first time my parents had seen my name and comments in print. When UPI appeared to be shutting down in the late Nineties, Dave moved on to the "religion and social issues" beat at the Religion News Service. He decided to retire in 2004 and his colleagues held a going away party before he left for Plentywood, Montana, a tiny outpost of civilization amidst farms and ranches just south of the Canadian border. His new home was marked by a small pin in a large map of the United States prominently displayed at his reception. His fellow journalists made one point again and again: "Dave was a seminal figure in creating the idea that you could have a full-time job covering religion." His writing spawned decisions at major radio and television networks and many local papers to hire religion beat reporters.

I had one final chat with Dave that night. He commented that, while packing up his things to move, he had come across a photograph someone had taken of him interviewing me at a rally to oppose the return of the military draft. Coincidentally, I had just found that photo myself. Almost simultaneously we said: "We sure had more hair then."

The Journalist's Journalist: Walter Cronkite

I had never actually met Walter Cronkite of *CBS News* until the spring of 2008 when my friend, the Rev. C. Welton Gaddy, and I were the "opening act" for an appearance Cronkite made at the Commonwealth Club in San Francisco. We were there to promote the First Freedom First project funded in large part by Intel founder Andy Grove.

What fascinated me the most was that Cronkite was so curious about what Welton and I had to say, particularly about the likely relationship between Governor Mitt Romney's Mormon beliefs and his governance, should he become the next President. Cronkite had no professional reason to get into this because he had retired in 1981 as the anchor of the evening news. He was just driven by intense curiosity, the basis for great journalism. Too many television hosts and anchors now seem to be hired for some combination of appearance and the ability to read from teleprompters. Cronkite had once been named one of the "best dressed men in America," to which he responded: "I'm behind a desk every night. How do they know I am even wearing pants?" Cronkite's reporting on the Vietnam War was so critical that even President Lyndon Johnson once bemoaned: "If I have lost Cronkite, I have lost the country," a reference to the enormous respect the public had for his journalistic integrity.

Cronkite retired from CBS and was replaced by Dan Rather, who was unceremoniously dropped by the network in 2006, after rightwing reporters made far too much of one gaffe he made in reporting.

When Reportage Goes Bad

"Sticks and stones can break my bones, but words can never hurt me" may be one of the dopiest aphorisms in the English language. So much hate mail came into Americans United that we created a Wall of Shame consisting of the worst of it. A sample: "I hope you and every member of your staff gets cancer" and "Fuck you people," signed by someone who declared himself, as so many haters did, to be a "Christian." Jordan Peele and Jane Lynch agreed to spend a Saturday in Los Angeles producing and starring in a video called *The Separation of Church and State* in which the two played a couple, decked out in Seventies regalia, deciding to get a divorce, singing a song written by Faith Soloway. Since I was scheduled to do a speech at the Community Church of Boston that night and preach in a Boston suburb the next day, I couldn't go to Los Angeles. To give them a hint of what Americans United's office was like, a person from our communications staff filmed me walking around commenting on some of the highlights of how we worked and pointing out the Wall of Shame. The hate mail even made an appearance at one of the Lynn family Halloween parties that we held most years. Pieces dangled from the costume of someone dressed like a wall.

This mail didn't bother me much, but every year or so someone on the AU staff would ask to chat with me about some particularly rancid piece of mail or, later, email that she or he had received. It did strike me that it must take a most unpleasant personality to send cancer wishes or call down the wrath of God on somebody you knew, at most, from a clip on the television news. I'm all for hating people's bad ideas or even whole groups—civil liberties jerks or white supremacists—but when it gets so personal, one wonders what the next step in their outrage might be. Sadly, the very day after I returned from Boston, there was the running of the Boston Marathon and the deadly bombing that killed three people and mutilated twenty others. One of the bombs went off in the same block as the Community Church of Boston, at which I had spoken.

I worried about the safety of people who worked with me. One of our employees, Adam Sarapa, had a relative who worked for the District of Columbia police. He gave us helpful advice about how to deal with the literal death threats we got. Apparently, there are fairly routine methods to determine if a voicemail threat from someone in Alaska that is repeated a few days later is in fact coming from some other state that would indicate that person was moving in your direction. We did hire security for months during the Ten Commandments legal battle in Alabama because our legal director at the time, Ayesha Khan, had gotten explicit threats after her one and only appearance on Fox News. The issue itself, combined with her Southern Asian name and appearance were enough to bring out the worst in critics.

Hate mail is one thing; erroneous press reports are a beast of another kind. There were four times that press reporting of what I said or did was profoundly wrong and deeply disturbing. Indeed, the second dopiest aphorism is "There is no such thing as bad press."

First up was a statement attributed to me on the front page of the *Washington Post* shortly before the 1976 election in which I was quoted saying that I "don't believe Jimmy Carter would follow through on his pledge to grant pardons to war resisters." This would have been big news since I was chairing that massive coalition of groups who wanted an amnesty and who knew that Carter was the best chance we'd ever had to get something close to it. I had said I believed Carter "*would* follow through" on his commitment—the opposite of the attributed front-page quotation. I got a lot of calls the morning it appeared from coalition members, members of Congress, and others about why I would say that, even if I believed it. I told them I was misquoted of course, but even with the next day's correction (on the second page along with a few other clarifications), there was a lot of explaining to do. But this was minor in comparison to a few other pieces of unpleasant press.

There was a long piece in the *Post* by Morton Mintz suggesting that the American Civil Liberties Union had taken a position in defense of advertising tobacco products because it received major grants from the tobacco industry. Since I was the First Amendment man for the ACLU in Washington, the allegation was that I had somehow benefited from this flow of cash. The ACLU was a supporter of protecting "commercial speech" long before any funding came from the smoking industry. I resented the implication that I was somehow "bought off" personally. Just to be absolutely clear: I had never received anything of value from any cigarette manufacturer or the industry's Washington lobbying office, the Tobacco Institute. I went through years of checkbook registers to be absolutely sure that no one from these places gave me a stipend or a fee for any speech I gave or article I wrote. I found nothing but a piece I had written for *Playboy* about why commercial speech should be protected that carried a few hundred dollars compensation.

I believe even now that the ACLU was correct in defense of the right to advertise any lawful product and to advocate for the legalization of currently illegal products. I did predict in Congressional testimony that cigarette advertising would soon be abandoned as a useless method of acquiring new smokers and that the industry would focus more on getting peer-to-peer smoking growth. That did happen. There is very little cigarette or cigar advertising left today— although vaping products are now advertised.

The worst example of journalistic error, though, occurred in early March of 1994 when I was doing a daily radio program with Pat Buchanan. When I got to the office my brilliant communications director Joe Conn asked me, "What the hell went wrong on the radio the other day?" I had not seen the paper yet and was horrified to see a column by respected writer Courtland Milloy about an interview I participated in with Buchanan and comedian Jackie Mason, who may at one time have been funny but was now just mean-spirited and offensive. Mason had said a number of racist things that I countered on the show, but the column said I had let him make vicious statements without challenge. And there were quotations from my purported interview to prove it. I soon realized that Mason had also been on the same radio station with another guy the same day, Bob Levey. Milloy had mixed up me with Bob.

When I did the radio show that day, Buchanan mentioned that he hadn't remembered me saying any of the things attributed to me and that the column was libelous. I said I was working on a correction. I reached out to my longtime friend and associate Wade Henderson, who had worked at the ACLU and was then head of the NAACP. As soon as he answered the phone, he mentioned that he had seen I had really ticked off Courtland. "That's what I am calling about because I never said any of those things. He has me confused with somebody else," I said.

Wade agreed to call Courtland immediately and Milloy called me a few hours later to apologize and note that there would be a similar apology in his next column. There was: it was a flattering statement of my civil rights work in the past and a fully repentant explanation of his error. When I did the radio that day, Buchanan gloated that it was a total recantation of Milloy's mistake.

Here are two more examples of the way in which printed and spoken words can cause long-lasting problems: Make something up and attribute it to somebody you don't like, or try to profit from a situation that you created by artifice. Make up a quote? For years, Pat Robertson said: "Barry Lynn even believes that if a church is on fire, the city fire department cannot put it out." This is a ridiculous idea that I have never heard anyone suggest. Even anti-religious people wouldn't take this position, if for no other reason than that the fire might spread to their favorite grocery store. But he repeated it regularly for years. Many reporters searched for where I might have said this but came up empty handed. Jen Hegerty, doing research for this book, found an entire Wikipedia entry devoted to Pat Robertson controversies and I was proud to see that this misstatement was one of them.

Profit from a misrepresented activity? Meet James White, the founder of Alpha and Omega Ministries. White is a traveling professional apologist for conservative Christianity who debates liberal theologians around the country. He called to see if I would like to debate the topic "Is Homosexuality Compatible with Authentic Christianity" at a church on Long Island.

I told him I would do it but wouldn't do it on behalf of Americans United because the organization had no official theological position. It supported LGBTQ+ rights as a matter of law and public policy. White assured me that would not be a problem and we started to outline the way the debate would occur. I had a few ground rules, the most important of which was that the audience members would have a chance to ask questions. He agreed.

I had gotten a call from a longtime friend, John C. Swomley, a few days before the debate. He said he had foolishly agreed to have a debate on abortion with White and that it was horrible, and I shouldn't debate him on any topic. I told John that I didn't feel comfortable declining at this late date and that the audience would have an opportunity to weigh in. I should have listened to Swomley. I got to the church a bit early and saw that it was almost completely full. It had been heavily advertised by the local Christian radio station and there were plenty of cars with "Christian" bumper sticks parked around the place: "Abortion Kills a Beating Heart" and "Evolution is a Lie." I met the radio host, Chris Arzen, who would introduce White and me. As we were walking up to the front of the church, Arzen said, "We have had to change plans. There will be no question period because we were concerned that ACT UP would disrupt the event." Of course, even seconds away from the debate, I should have told him that I wouldn't participate since audience involvement was a condition of my participation in the first place. I merely said I was disappointed in the change.

I got a lot more than disappointed shortly thereafter. White was one of the most hateful opponents I ever met, arrogant and smug, mean-spirited and obnoxious. He expressed many times during the nearly two hours of debate equivalents of the statement: "I hate the sin, not the sinner," but I didn't believe it for one minute. As my closing argument time came, I noted: "Well, you folks have been watching me for two hours, but maybe you forget that I have been watching you too. I have never seen an audience so full of hate as you folks." They were all upset, with one woman in the front row literally wailing as if I had sent a demon (which I am quite sure she believed were real) to possess her. There was a small contingent of gay people who were sitting in the back and whose demands to be heard were ignored. The security for the night was a Christian motorcycle gang who were prepared to do whatever it took to prevent any more outbursts.

I was so disappointed that I hadn't walked back down the center aisle as soon as the moderator told me of his change of plans. I wrote him that I "considered that an inexcusable breach of trust... since I got to the event early, you could have told me then and we could have discussed it with the church pastor...If he had not been able to re-adjust, I would probably have left." I continued that the evening had been "a thoroughly distasteful event and I will certainly encourage other 'liberals' and persons of good will to ignore your series, The Great Debate, like the plague. You have a wonderful little racket going. Going where, I would rather not say." I copied James White on this message, to which he responded that I owed Arnzen a strong apology because "scholarly debates" never have a question and answer period. If that were true (it is not), they should never have agreed on that model in the first place. As I was driving back to the hotel, I even called my friend Alan Colmes who was doing his late-night syndicated radio show to mention the incident. I got a little sleep and flew home. Even that was not the end of the matter.

A few days later, my communications team noticed that the Alpha and Omega Ministries website now contained a video of the debate that could be purchased for $25. I had never agreed to allow the distribution of this product since this was "my work" and I didn't want these haters to benefit financially from this discourse. I wrote a letter of objection to White, who responded that he thought it was ridiculous that a First Amendment free speech advocate would try to "censor" his own words. White also put out press releases about my "censorship." Cal Thomas, who had worked for Jerry Falwell and then became the second most popular syndicated conservative columnist (second only to George Will) got one of those press releases. We used to do a lot of radio and television appearances together and, when I explained that I don't even allow friendly audiences to tape and distribute my speeches, it took him a nanosecond to tell me he did the same and wouldn't print anything about the White controversy.

I ended up spending $10,000 on a Los Angeles lawyer who filed a claim on my behalf. Eventually I won $1 and an agreement that the product would no longer be sold. It was a Pyrrhic victory, but the idea of trying to get a cut of the proceeds seemed way too costly and the video had already been uploaded to YouTube. A year or so later, when I told this story to one of the best lawyers I know in Washington, he said: "I wish you had just called me. I would have had my firm do this pro bono and we would put that guy out of business." I guess sometimes you really ought to reach out to your friends for help.

Chapter 7

MY OWN "RADIO DAZE": PARTICIPATING IN OPINIONATED RADIO

Many people of my era listened to their transistor radios carefully concealed under their pillows when they were teens. Until late in high school, I only enjoyed instrumental music–too many 101 Strings records in my parents' record collection–and talk radio. There was something extremely exciting about listening to shows from New York City, static included.

My two favorite hosts were "Long John" Nebel and Joe Pyne. Nebel mostly discussed the weird and supernatural. Hours were filled with discourse on the Abominable Snowman, psychic powers like telekinesis, ghosts, and UFOs. I consider all this total malarkey now, but at the time, I was riveted by Nebel's guests and their frequent claims that the government knew about all this but was seeking to cover it up.

Pyne was of a whole different order. I was a conservative young person and, like Hillary Clinton, even sported a "Goldwater for President" pin in 1964. Pyne was a rightwinger's rightwinger. I was a tad uncomfortable with how he savaged his guests and any callers who disagreed with him, but occasionally he did the right thing. During one of his interviews of George Lincoln Rockwell, then head of the American Nazi Party, he noted that Rockwell's conservative views were anti-American and signed off: "George, go gargle with razor blades."

Aside from a brief stint on college radio playing folk music and doing a satirical show, I never thought I would have an opportunity to host a show, but I was delighted during my anti-war and civil liberties days to be a guest on talk shows. After the publicity I got battling the Meese Commission, a start-up company approached me. They were eager to enter the lucrative Washington DC radio market with "personality driven" talk radio and had purchased a small AM radio station, WNTR, in Silver Spring, Maryland. I got a call from somebody named Jeff Botkin whose personal fashion statement seemed to be always wearing a stopwatch around his neck. He asked, "Would you want to test for being the co-host of show called *Battleline*?" It would be modeled after Tom Braden and Pat Buchanan's *Crossfire*, which had been a radio hit on another Washington, DC station but had recently moved to CNN. It became clear that the right side of the argument was to be handled by either conservative movement icon Howard Phillips or *Washington Times* columnist John Lofton, both men with ultraconservative political and religious views. (Phillips later went on to run for president on the Constitution Party ticket, receiving several hundred thousand votes in 2000.)

My first try-out was with Lofton. We discussed religion in schools and the death penalty. "Discuss" was probably too polite a description of what occurred. He was a screamer of unparalleled tenacity. He would invariably start a conversation asking a few seemingly thoughtful questions and then plummet into harangues, accusations, vocal escalation, and a general rudeness, which is today copied only on radio by Michael Savage. I felt there was nothing to lose by being more belligerent than usual because I considered it inconceivable that anyone would hire Lofton to do anything that required him to open his mouth. The tryout seemed to go well.

I was invited back a few days later to spar with Howard Phillips. He insisted on changing seats between hours so he would face the interior of the building the first hour and the outside window during the second hour. I didn't know why. The first hour was a lively (but infinitely more genteel than either hour with Lofton) interchange about the newly uncovered AIDS epidemic. Phillips was in favor of immediate quarantine; I was in favor of spending as much as it took to find the cause and develop a cure. At the newsbreak between hours, Phillips got up to move to where I was sitting but insisted I take the windscreen covering my microphone and switch it with his.

He obviously was afraid that since I was speaking up for gay people, and gay people and Haitians were the groups identified as most likely to contract the illness, I might be gay and could even have AIDS. Since he was convinced that this virus could remain live for days, it might leap from my windscreen to his mouth and infect him. I figured that we would have to maintain a pretty rigid seating arrangement if we ended up together, because I would rather grab a Coke at the break than spend the time changing windscreens.

The team the company chose was John Lofton and me. We were scheduled to do 4 to 6 p.m. weekdays. My ACLU employers thought it was a good idea for me to try this. A radio expert named Ed Graham was hired to run the whole shebang. We were scheduled to start one Monday in May, but Lofton didn't show up until close to 5 p.m. For that first hour affable Ed Graham sat in the opposite chair, and we started chatting about the right against self-incrimination and pumped the new telephone number just in case somebody had tapped into the new signal and desperately wanted to chat about the Fifth Amendment—I don't even remember why we were discussing it and nobody called in.

When Lofton arrived, he was angry about the "time change" (there hadn't been one) and never gave up his hostility until the day we were both fired. He was also furious about our pay scale and a few days later in a more reasonable chat with management, I convinced them to give us more compensation. How angry a man was John Lofton? One day during a discussion of affirmative action, which he hated, an African American caller took offense at his views and after the screaming went on for a few minutes, Lofton actually invited the caller to come down to the parking lot and settle things. We cut to commercial with the caller ready to return and I suggested he tone things down. Lofton said, "He'll never show up." Unpersuaded by his apparent psychic power to foretell the future, I reintroduced the show and said to the caller that if he wanted to come down, I was the guy in the suit and Lofton was the fellow with the bushy, anarchist-like beard. Fearing that the caller would use the stereotypical appearances of people on the left and right, I didn't want to take the chance of ending up in the emergency room by mistake. The caller never did show up.

On another occasion, Lofton was screeching at a grandmother who was discussing her gay grandson and the wonderful new organization she was helping to start called Parents and Friends of Lesbians and Gays (PFLAG). He hurled Scripture at her, called her and her grandson immoral, referred to gays as perverts, and did so in such a shockingly rude manner that a person called the police department and said a madman had taken over WNTR. When the police called the station, they were informed that "that was just our regular talent." The police didn't show up either.

I used to do things on Lofton's day off that I knew would irritate him. When Yippie leader and author of *Steal This Book*, Abbie Hoffman, was on the run from federal authorities on a drug charge, he would sometimes arrange with me to call into the show, and I always loved chatting with him solo. On one occasion, Hoffman was discussing marijuana legalization, which I said was obviously a good idea, but then I said we should do the same for most other then illicit drugs. During a break, he told the producer that I was the most leftwing talk show host he ever spoke to because of my support for near total drug legalization. The next time Lofton was present, he berated me for again talking to Hoffman without him. Hoffman had surgery to change his appearance and changed his name to Barry Freed. Eventually despondent over the failure of the Movement's protest culture to grow, Hoffman committed suicide in his Pennsylvania apartment at age 52 after swallowing 150 tablets of phenobarbital.

Lofton was so belligerent that those two hours were often the worst of my day, no matter what else had happened. A consultant hired to syndicate the show managed only to get it on in Richmond, Virginia, and then only when baseball was not being aired. Then the consultant suddenly disappeared. Shortly thereafter, after ugly but apparently true reports of tax fraud by one of the owners surfaced, the whole station went dark. Ironically, the only time I felt that I had any human, decent connection to Lofton was when I explained how we could work together, to get our last paycheck from the company. Presuming that since I was a lawyer, I knew something about how to receive earned but unpaid salary, he agreed to come with me to the office to get that final paycheck. It worked, but I rarely saw Lofton again. When he was fired from the *Washington Times* for blowing the whistle on a sexual harassment incident at the paper, and his departure was announced, the entire newsroom erupted in applause. He went on to host a show on a tiny Maryland station, sell a Reconstructionist newsletter for a few hundred dollars a year, tried to launch a debate show on a Laurel, Maryland, public access channel, and got himself excommunicated from his local church. He died in 2014 of a heart condition.

Despite this experience, I had the bug for radio as a way to change a few minds. My next opportunity came from the unlikeliest of sources: the Rev. Pat Robertson. Robertson had gone from owning a single radio station in Virginia to developing an international television empire. He thought what America needed was a secular, conservative radio network from coast to coast. In a strategy developed by Rush Limbaugh, Robertson would find some small stations outside of a major market and then hope that his ratings would rise sufficiently to get into the city directly on some major station. And he had plenty of cash behind him.

I was approached by someone in the Robertson empire to co-host a show on WNTR that Pat had purchased. My co-host was Pat Korten, a former CBS radio anchor in Washington who was talented and legitimately conservative without being crazy like Lofton. This show was so much more fun to do than my previous one, and Robertson thought it should again be called *Battleline*. Korten was a genuinely fun guy to work with and we talked to all kinds of people—politicians, pundits, scientists, movie stars, and occasional strange people who hit the news only once because of some odd thing that happened to them. It was produced by one man who was a religious conservative. He was at work early every morning to line up guests before many of the bookers for other shows had even gotten out of bed. I've always thought he was so successful because when he'd introduce himself as from NTR (News Talk Radio network) the person he was calling heard it as "NPR" (National Public Radio). There were certain topics that we were each particularly sensitive about and we just skipped them.

I had fun. How could one not enjoy a few of these programs? Once we interviewed the neighbor of Zsa Zsa Gabor, a siren of Sixties cinema, who went to court to force Ms. Gabor to cut down a tree whose roots were growing so long that they had cracked his driveway. The only problem was that the fellow had severe memory impairment. On the air he claimed not to remember that he had even been to court the day before. He called out to his spouse, and we could hear her in the background assuring him that the two of them had indeed been in court over the tree root incident.

We interviewed a lawyer for a supermarket chain sued by a man who slipped on a peapod. For over six minutes he explained how the chain store determined whether a fallen vegetable had leaked enough moisture to create a potential slipping hazard. I was laughing so hard I could hardly terminate the interview for a commercial.

In another memorable incident, Korten was late for the show, and I conducted an interview by myself with a member of Congress who was one of Pat's friends. Without acknowledging Pat wasn't there, I kept saying things like: "Well, Congressman, your friend Pat is eating this up, but I'm not buying it."

I once asked Republican Congressman Tom Campbell of California, who had just been named by *Roll Call* as the smartest member of the House, if he was so smart, could he tell me the square root of 1492. He took it in the proper spirit. Campbell left Congress to become the dean of the law school at Chapman University in California. I was later introduced to him by my host at a speech there, told him that story, and he laughed, noting that it was a good story but he couldn't remember it happening.

When the show was being aired in New Orleans, we thought it would be useful to have interviews with two people running for Governor at the time, a Democrat named Edwin Edwards and the white supremacist former head of the Ku Klux Klan, the flamboyant David Duke. The Democrat was eager to appear and was booked, but there had been no response from Duke. During the interview, none other than Duke himself called into the station after listening to the show on his car radio. He asked to be put on after the next commercial, which we did. He began by saying, "I don't object to you having my opponent on, I just wanted equal time." My response was "Well, that is real white of you, but we asked you hours ago and you ignored the request." Korten blanched at the comment and my reference to Duke's "whiteness," but he didn't mention it until the interview was finished.

The only truly bad on-air incident occurred on one of the rare days that Korten took off. His substitute was Cliff Kincaid who had his own show and who was a writer for *Human Events*, an ultraconservative weekly newspaper. Our guest was former Senator George McGovern. Although the conversation started friendly enough, Cliff soon started to needle McGovern over some of the planks in his 1972 Presidential campaign. McGovern valiantly defended his position, and then Kincaid, in a reference to McGovern's recently failed effort to open a bed and breakfast in Connecticut, said "It is a good thing we didn't trust the American economy to somebody who can't run a hotel." McGovern had acquired the leasehold for a place called the Stratford Inn in 1988 but it had enormous financial difficulties which he had explained in a l992 article in the *Wall Street Journal*. He noted in that piece that he had wished he had a better understanding of the needs of small businesses when he was in the Senate, that "one-size-fits-all rules...ignore the reality of the marketplace." He wished he "had known more about the hazards and difficulties of such a business, especially during a recession of the kind that hit New England just as he was acquiring it."

McGovern didn't hang up, but I had to call him during the news break to apologize for Kincaid's generally mean-spirited actions. Cliff Kincaid later made national news when he referred to television personality Connie Chung as "Connie Chink." He later "apologized," but only "if anyone was offended." Say, the entire Asian American population of the nation?

Although Pat Robertson often prefers to be characterized as a Christian businessman, instead of a television preacher, and although he has more money than God using any standard accounting procedure, the News Talk Radio network was one of his biggest financial failures. It didn't help that a fire gutted the studios in Silver Spring one Friday night, possibly caused by the overnight host smoking, but the company had built out a new studio in the offices of the Christian Broadcasting Network in time for Korten and me to go on the air Monday afternoon at four o'clock. This seemed to be a sign that the company was in it for the long haul, but it was not. Indeed, just weeks after the network manager, Michael DelGiorno, had called me into his office to ask, "Can you handle earning a million dollars next year?" and after thousands of expensive network brochures had been sent to thousands of radio stations, something went seriously awry.

Bill Trombley, the fellow responsible for affiliate relations showed me a stack of literally hundreds of pink WHILE YOU WERE OUT forms on his table, all a result of the promotional mailing, then asked me to close the door, and told me that for unknown reasons he had been ordered not to return any of the calls. His office was engulfed in boxes containing dedicated satellite receivers that could be used to pick up the NTR signal virtually anywhere in the country, even if stations were too poor to have a mobile satellite dish.

I was not a businessman, but if you have tens of thousands of dollars' worth of hardware to give to stations gratis for picking up your shows, and you had hundreds of program managers and station owners responding to a single mailing, that sounded like a clarion call to move ahead, not sit on your hands. I would have been right in most universes, but in the Pat Robertson astral plane, such logic failed.

Although the full story of NTR may never be known, allegations of massive employee theft came to light. It was rumored that the whole operation had lost as much as eight million dollars one way or the other. Although the network kept *Battleline* going for a few months longer than its other shows, it was clearly doomed.

We had a few affiliates still left. Korten and I had formed our own company and arranged for NTR to allow us to use its facilities for free. However, we had no money to promote the show and what little we had was drying up fast. One Friday we decided to can the whole gig.

That Sunday, there was a shakeup in the Chinese government. I was in New York that weekend to get some award, and Korten called me frantically on Monday morning to ask if, in light of the "China situation," we should hang on one more week. I tried to break the news gently, "Pat, I don't think our fans in Albuquerque give a shit what we think about China."

My next foray into talk shows was with Pat Buchanan on his syndicated radio show *Pat Buchanan and Company* on the Mutual Broadcasting System. I was not an original member of the "company" when it began on July 5, 1993, but within weeks the originals, including Chris Matthews, Bob Beckel, and Juan Williams, had become so disenchanted that they left the show. The show's booker was Dianne Robinson, known widely as having the "best Rolodex of guests in Washington." She suggested to her boss that he give me a shot. One July morning I showed up to debate Buchanan about three issues I knew very little about. However, Dianne prepared packets of material for Pat and his co-host that were short, pithy, and fact filled. My "audition" went so well that I was immediately hired to join the rotation. I soon became the sole counterpoint.

I always made it a point to arrive early to absorb Dianne's brilliantly crafted materials as I consumed the balanced lunch of two chili dogs and a large Coke. Once when discussing some food safety issue. Pat retuned from a commercial break by noting, "Barry sounds like he is an expert on this, but he got all of his information on this subject by reading a *USA TODAY* editorial over lunch." (Such comments are a "no-no" among co-hosts who keep such thoughts unspoken.)

I was also late one day around Christmas—only breathlessly arriving at the studio a minute before airtime as Pat quipped: "Where have you been? Kicking over Nativity scenes?" Joanne and Nick took a weeklong vacation to visit Alaska and Nick had dozed off in the backseat of a rental car when the show came on. Nick woke up and said: "That's Dad!"

I was then having daily radio debates with Pat Buchanan. I heard from some of his political allies all kinds of ridiculous claims. Senator Bob Smith (R/NH) told me that parents had informed him that obscene books were being used in high school sex education classes. The Senator conceded that none of his constituents had actually found such a book in the Granite State, but they had heard they were used in New York. One of Pat's favorite authors told us there was secret testing going on in public schools as part of a widespread effort to indoctrinate kids, a precursor to implanting microchips in the children to record personal data about morals and family life. When I told Pat that, in our daughter's high school, some parents wanted to eliminate Edgar Allan Poe's "The Telltale Heart" from literature classes, he replied that Poe's "The Black Cat," was too horrible for anyone to read before college.

Occasionally when I had access to the sizable audience of *Pat Buchanan and Company*–heard on about 100 stations and closing in on the audience of competitor Rush Limbaugh in a few markets–I would try to make news myself. For example, I tried to end the policy of paying two chaplains for Congress roughly $288,000. The Senate chaplain at the time was Richard C. Halverson, who got $115,700 and was about to retire after serving there for fourteen years. His House counterpart received $123,000. Pay for their staffs made up the other $50,000. The new Republican leadership promised to be fiscally conservative and had announced they were going to fire the Congressional elevator operators. On the show in early January 1995, I had a chance to ask the second-ranking Republican, Louisiana's Bob Livingston, if he might think about replacing the taxpayer funded chaplains with local volunteers. I was pleasantly surprised when he said such a move was being considered.

Literally hundreds of churches, synagogues, and mosques are near the Capitol, along with dozens of clergy who worked at the so-called DC God Box where I had worked years before for the United Church of Christ. Although a poorly analyzed decision by the Supreme Court in 1983 upheld the concept of a paid chaplain as constitutional, nothing suggested that a volunteer, free chaplaincy would not be a good substitute. I preferred the thinking of James Madison, who when he left Congress and the Presidency, wrote that, upon reflection, the paid chaplaincy was a "national establishment of religion" and that, if Congresspersons wanted a chaplain, they should pay for them out of their own pockets. He wrote, "How just would it be in its principle!" One of Madison's concerns was that an inequality of representation in the chaplaincy would arise. Indeed, by 1995, every chaplain to Congress had been a white male Protestant, except for a Catholic priest who served briefly in the mid-19th century.

Iowa Representative Jim Nussle, active in the Republican majority transition, had already indicated that he was exploring using volunteers, which had been done for six years just before the Civil War. The job of chaplain consisted mainly of giving an opening prayer each morning, with almost no Members attending, and providing spiritual guidance when Members were in crisis. Congresswoman Bella Abzug once asked me to do the opening prayer. I declined, since I don't think a prayer should open legislative activities.

For a while, the stars were aligning to save the money, increase the diversity of prayers, and be faithful to Madisonian principles. Then Newt Gingrich got wind of what Livingston had said. Gingrich acknowledged to *The New York Times* that it had been considered and rejected because "it might look like we didn't care about religion." If some Congressional action looked bad toward religion, conventional political wisdom held it to be political suicide. I wondered what would happen the day that Gingrich got his proposed school prayer amendment to the floor and *TIME* magazine noted that there were vastly more votes for it than the number of Members who were on that floor for the morning prayer.

The United Auto Workers Union had been convinced to buy a fledgling radio network to promote Democratic and Republican populism. The union hired a man named Cliff Curley, whose prior job had been selling videotapes about flying saucers. It was not a success, although I did spend about a year on a show called *Newsmaker*, a one-hour late afternoon gabfest hosted by Michelle Laxalt, the daughter of Senator Paul Laxalt (R/NV). She was a conventional Republican, not as crazed as John Lofton, and probably even a bit more open-minded than Pat Korten. She ran a lobbying firm and had lots of heavy-hitter Republican friends like John Bolton who'd come into the Capitol Hill studios and then hang around after the show to chat.

Lynn does his daily radio program **Cultureshocks** *interviewing intelligent people about politics, religion, and science.*

Years later, I began doing radio again while at Americans United, this time four or five hours a week, mainly recorded to be aired late in the afternoon on a handful of stations. The show was called *Cultureshocks* and was originally created and produced by a very talented woman from our communications department named Donya Khalili. The purpose of the show was to chat with people who were not generally engaged with church/state issues but who would be good at promoting critical thinking, scientific work, constitutional theory, or who just wrote about topics I found intriguing. Doing this show kept me alert to the world and gave me a chance to pontificate on non-religious liberty issues, which in turn made me a better guest on the regular radio and television shows on which I appeared. I had favorite guests of course, including Mary Roach, who wrote a new book every few years, each with a single word title that included *Stiff* (about cadavers), *Spook* (about science and the afterlife), and *Bonk* (about science and sex). Every time Charles Manson prosecutor Vincent Bugliosi wrote a book, I would have him on. With most authors, I had generally read the book we would be discussing. But I conceded to Vince that his monumental examination of the John Kennedy assassination, which was 1632 pages long and came with a CD-ROM including an additional 1000 pages, was one I had not had a chance to read in anything close to its entirety. He also wrote a book exploring the evidence for and against the existence of God but concluded that that he did not know the answer.

Chapter 8

PODCASTING

After recovering from months in hospitals in 2019, I was eager to return to something like normalcy, I thought podcasting was the way to go. Everyone was doing it and with my background in radio, I thought it would be easy.

One of the radio owners who played *Cultureshocks* was Fred Lundgren who had, among other things, worked with the brilliant progressive Texan, former Texas Agriculture Commissioner Jim Hightower. Hightower and I had both been on that network operated by the United Autoworkers Union (called for reasons I never fully understood, "i.e., America"), me occasionally filling in for him when he was on vacation. Jim was known for many aphorisms, my favorite being, "The only things in the middle of the road are yellow stripes and dead skunks." I was live on Jim's show only once when I was fundraising in Austin, Texas, but it was great fun and I could easily see how Jim and Fred could have gotten along.

Fred was an extraordinary, driven man, convinced that quality radio broadcasting can have a major impact on the political scene. I had enjoyed broadcasting on his California radio station, KCAA in Riverside, California, just south of Los Angeles. He liked my show and after my retirement, he urged me to rejoin the programming on KCAA and two other small FM stations he had acquired in Southern California. I would become part of his podcasting world as well.

I had never listened to podcasts but was intrigued by the idea and the relatively modest cost of becoming a part of that universe. About a year after my heart hospitalizations, I had created a website *http://cultureshocks.com* and read a few books on the topic while spending a week at Joanne's brother's place on a lake in Minnesota.

Every podcast (and there were then over 700,000 of them) needs to have a theme of some kind and I thought I had a great one: have guests whom I thought were not sufficiently recognized for the work they do. My "elevator pitch" was, "David Letterman has a podcast called 'My Next Guest Needs No Introduction' and he has really famous people on it. My podcast is based on the premise: 'If the world was fair, my next guest wouldn't need an introduction, but since the world isn't, she does.'" It would feature people I had admired. In many cases, they would be people I had met during my work life who didn't get the credit I thought—and presumably they thought—they deserved. Fred encouraged me to keep the title of my old radio show *Cultureshocks* and I did.

This podcast lasted about a year. When it worked, it was really fun and guests had a good time doing it. The problem was, it didn't always work. There were technical problems of gigantic proportions which included bad telephones, forgotten appointments, time zone screwups, and difficulties in editing the shows, in spite of the valiant efforts of Fred's son who prepared the shows for broadcast, inserting music and cuts from comedy albums when the guest was a musician or comic.

I enjoyed the opportunity to chat with people I respected in the worlds of music, comedy, and political activism. Many of them seemed eager to appear on the show, even though it was unlikely that their appearances would lead to either more fame or greater fortune.

Many of the comedians were folks I had met on panels for John Fuegelsang's shows: Liz Miele, Mark Ramirez, Krystal Kamenides, Rhonda Hansome, and Leah Bonnema. Leah had gotten a break appearing on *The Late Show with Steven Colbert*. In earlier times, this would launch a career to atmospheric heights, but these days, it apparently doesn't work that way. She is a horror movie fan and I still regularly give her recommendations for what she might enjoy. Mark and Krystal were considering launching their own podcast and are "foodies" of some renown. During their appearance on

Cultureshocks, I mentioned that, although I wasn't a connoisseur of food, my daughter had, for several years, made a square Christmas cookie with sprinkles of the words Free Snoop, a reference to the release of the incarcerated rapper Snoop Doggy Dogg.

Activists who had few opportunities to appear anywhere in the mainstream media had a place at my table. The Tor Project encouraged people to use the highly private Tor browser which contains levels of encryption unheard of in regular access to the internet. Although the so-called "dark web" is usually vilified as a sanctuary for hitmen, child pornography producers, and gunrunners, my guest explained all the useful purposes it serves. Tor allows human rights dissidents around the world to communicate safely without fear of discovery by government officials who would try to locate, imprison, and in some cases kill them. Women who are being stalked or are victims of spousal abuse often need extremely secure ways to communicate and Tor provides that as well.

I had time and space for other groups that did great work for oppressed and injured people. The Woodhull Freedom Forum, named after the first woman to run for president and early feminist, Virginia Woodhull, advocated for sexual freedom as a human right and presented the opportunity to interview a labor organizer whose work was now focused on organizing sex workers. Elizabeth Anne Wood had written a book about her mother's hospitalization experiences called *Bound*, because her mother had been a professional dominatrix. The book explored the unique medical challenges that profession presented but was also a scathing critique of the American healthcare system for all of us.

One of my musical guests, Jaimee Harris, talked about her struggles with addiction, which led to an interview with the director of the innovative treatment program called the SIMS Foundation in Austin, Texas, that had brought her recovery.

I loved chatting with musicians who did not get the recognition I thought they deserved. Grant Peeples is a Florida songwriter who had never performed publicly until he was 40 and who I first met at a Folk Alliance International Conference in Memphis when he had Jaimee Harris in his band. Others included Liz Barnez of Colorado, who was a good friend of Catie Curtis, and Anne Hills, whose beautiful voice had mesmerized me for years. Hills was also a therapist now living in my hometown of Bethlehem, Pennsylvania.

I was also glad to have a visit from James Reston, Jr., right after he recovered the diary he had done during the summer of 1974 as Richard Nixon's presidency was collapsing. We spoke about his work preparing British television host David Frost for his historic interviews with Nixon that aired on CBS in 1977. Frost's interview about Watergate was the most widely viewed television show in history because people wondered just what Nixon would say.

I interviewed the head of an improvisational comedy troupe from Minnesota. I had been a guest for their one and only trip to Washington, DC to do a few shows. Tane Danger is an extremely talented leader of this troupe and, unlike some improv groups I've seen, his folks seemed to take seriously the answers I was giving during the interview section of the performance. They built the comedy around those answers, unlike some groups that mainly seem to have bits lined up in advance that they can slip into so-called "improv" ideas that come from their audience. Tane liked my story about Reston's preparation for the Nixon interview because he remembered it as an influential piece of television he watched as a young man.

Reston also asked me if I'd like to read the draft of his impeachment diary. It was finally published and provides great background to the 2020 impeachment drive against Donald Trump. In Nixon's case, his doom was sealed when tape recordings of Oval Office exchanges were released and even formerly loyal Republicans turned on him. With Trump, of course, there were few anti-Trump voices in the entire Republican Party during his impeachment trials.

Chapter 9

FEMINISM AND ANTI-FEMINISTS

The issue of pornography divided feminists, but not their clear support for a woman's right to choose to have an abortion. Indeed, that was the issue that propelled me into work on separation of church and state.

Although I was troubled as a high school student about mandated prayer and Bible reading in my public school primarily because one of my closest friends who was Jewish said he was bothered by it, it was not until college that the intensity of my passion for religious liberty flourished.

I had a classmate in 1968, during my sophomore year, who was going to England for spring break. One evening I said: "That sounds like fun" to which he replied, "It won't be—my girlfriend is pregnant. We are going there to get an abortion." I was stunned. When I asked why he wasn't getting the procedure done here, he said no states permitted it. Even otherwise progressive jurisdictions like Massachusetts and New York had such powerful Catholic lobbies that the procedure remained illegal, thus their foreign travel.

I was utterly confused by the idea that any church could have this level of political clout in the United States. As I looked into this further, I discovered that contraception for married couples had been outlawed in many states before the seminal Supreme Court decision in *Griswold v. Connecticut* in 1965, and it took until 1972 for the Supreme Court to uphold the right for unmarried persons to obtain birth control in *Eisenstadt v. Baird*. The legalization of abortion (at least through the first six months of pregnancy) did not occur until 1973's *Roe v. Wade* decision. No wonder my roommate and his partner had to travel across the Atlantic Ocean.

It seemed like a no-brainer that a church should not have this much clout, particularly about something as intimate as a decision about whether to prevent pregnancy or carry a pregnancy to term. William Baird was the person who brought the issue of contraceptives for non-married couples to the Supreme Court. He was challenging his arrest for distributing condoms after a speech on contraception he had delivered at Boston University. This lawsuit was immensely controversial. Planned Parenthood did not initially support contraceptives for people not married and even the Massachusetts ACLU affiliate would not represent him directly. His counsel was Senator Joseph D. Tydings and the case was won by a 6-1 margin at the Supreme Court.

This whole college incident solidified my commitment to reproductive justice and the absolute right of a woman to make up her own mind about contraception and abortion. I originally had some qualms about the moral issues for myself, but they dissipated quickly after the incident with my classmate and have never returned. Americans United did not have a position on reproductive justice until I got there, but I insisted that we move into support soon after I arrived.

If you are a First Amendment "free speech" purist, you have to be able to tolerate lots of hateful commentary, but you also have to remind speakers that because of the very power of words, they should be selected carefully. I made that point to the convention of the American Humanist Association in June in Las Vegas when I received their annual Religious Liberty Award, noting that Pastor Wiley Drake had said that prayer had helped rid the nation of Dr. George Tiller, a physician providing abortions in Kansas. "No, Pastor Drake, it was not prayers that killed him; it was a man who listened to the rantings of people like you who provided him with the amoral framework to justify his actions." The killer was Scott Roeder, who had made occasional postings on rightwing websites but was not a leader of any anti-choice movement. This did not mean that every person associated with an anti-choice view should be hauled into the local FBI headquarters, but prudent investigative steps should be made. Just one day after I made these points in my "Beliefnet blog" on the *Washington Post* website, an 88-year-old man long associated with anti-Semitic hate groups walked into the Holocaust Memorial Museum in Washington firing a weapon and killing a security guard before being shot himself. He had told friends that he blamed Jews for electing Obama and that Jews were not "God's chosen." Presumably he considered himself to be in that august category.

In 2000 the Feminist Majority Foundation held a big gathering in Baltimore, appropriately called the Feminist Expo. One Saturday I was on a panel on the Religious Right. Since I was only one of five men in the overall agenda of three hundred speakers, I felt a particular burden not to mess up, particularly not to go over my five-minute limit. Mark Twain had often been asked to give speeches and he would always insist on knowing exactly how long they wanted him to talk. He claimed this was important because if the speech was for an hour, it would take him a day to write; if it was to last only 10 minutes, it would take him a month to write. I was still working on my five-minute presentation hours before the event.

Central to the presentation was a quote from Pat Robertson, who said in decrying feminism that it is a "socialist, anti-family political movement that encourages women to leave their husbands, kill their children, practice witchcraft, destroy capitalism, and become lesbians." After that I said: "And hearing that, I immediately signed up for the Feminist Majority Foundation." As my co-panelists were chatting before the panel began, one of them. Cecile Richards, mentioned to me that she was going to use that quote and I commented that it was more or less the cornerstone of my five minutes. She said, "Use it, I have lots of other things I can say." Cecile had recently taken the helm of Planned Parenthood and was a wildly popular speaker who could read the phone book and be revered, and I was not a well-known guy (and I was a white guy) so I was extremely thankful that she let me use the Robertson quote. Our presentations went over extremely well.

March for Women's Lives button, where Lynn
spoke before 1 million people.

In 2004, one million people attended the March for Women's Lives in Washington, and I was given a two-minute slot to speak, for which I was incredibly honored. My slot was right before lunch and followed Senator Hillary Clinton. The emcee just mentioned the name "Americans United for Separation of Church and State" and there was thunderous applause. Perhaps I should not say anything to dampen the moment, but that idea disappeared quickly. Here is the heart of what I had to say.

> *The Religious Right is out there trying to collapse the wall of separation between church and state, to crush anyone who does not see the world the way it does. And if they succeed, we will enter a Falwellian Dark Age where state-sponsored religion replaces responsible moral choice. We'll wake up to a nation where comprehensive sex education is censored, and we just pray that ignorance doesn't kill our children. Our country's laws could be based on Pat Robertson's messages from God, not on the liberties secured by our Constitution.*

The Religious Right's leaders are the people who contemptibly proclaimed that pro-choice Americans caused the attacks of September 11. They are neither smart enough nor moral enough to dare impose their vision on all of America. On this Sunday morning, this is hallowed space. This is a place where every child is a wanted child. This is where every woman's moral choice trumps the will of politicians and TV preachers.

Our current President says that he wants to cut funding for social programs but does want to spend money to go to Mars. On this latter point, I say, "Let him go there."

This is where we honor the struggles of our mothers and promote the dreams of our daughters by committing ourselves to protecting women's lives by protecting women's choices. In 2004, pessimism is death. Dr. Martin Luther King, Jr. reminded us that the arc of change is long, but it bends toward justice. We will soon step off on this historic march to help guarantee that justice, once achieved, will never be rolled back. The only way we lose it is if we quit. Will you be quitting?

That final question was not rhetorical. A resounding "no" was shouted to me on stage. As I walked off, Congresswoman Sheila Jackson Lee (D/TX) came up to me to say she loved my speech. Later in the day I saw people selling T-shirts with an image of George Bush on a rocket ship heading to Mars. If I had just thought of that! That evening I was at a folk music club in Northern Virginia and sitting by myself at a table near the stage. A family came in and asked if they could sit down. Of course I said yes. The father then said he thought he recognized me from one of the giant TV screens that had been placed on the Mall to air the march. I said that it was me but didn't know exactly what to expect since some "anti-choice" zealots had been in the crowd. I needn't have worried. He simply smiled and asked: "Can I buy you a cup of coffee?"

This was one of the most exhilarating events I ever participated in and sharing it with a million people was incredibly powerful. The only bad news came five months later when George W. Bush was re-elected by defeating a fine candidate, John Kerry of Massachusetts.

Bush accepted Kerry's concession but then called for an end to division in America: "We have one country, one Constitution and one future that binds us." Relevant post-election data showed that the Religious Right's hot button issues were not high on voters' minds, but that the war in Iraq, terrorism, and national security were what propelled Bush to victory and that the misleading attacks on Kerry's service in Vietnam had been highly successful at besmirching his reputation. His vote for and equivocation about the Iraq War didn't help.

Occasionally rightwing women claim the mantle of feminism. They claim they are pro-women. I'll discuss them first.

Phyllis Schlafly was the mother of anti-feminism and the subject of a 2020 cable series *Mrs. America,* starring Cate Blanchett. I first heard of her when she penned the consummate biography of Republican Presidential candidate Barry Goldwater called *Conscience of a Conservative*. At this point, I was still a political conservative, so I ate up that book, along with other tomes at the time like John Stormer's *None Dare Call It Treason*. I never expected to meet Phyllis, but that is the story of my life: no expectations, plenty of realities, most of them curious, even if not pleasant.

When CNN started, Ted Turner hired many of the correspondents from local radio station WTOP, Washington DC's sole all-news station at the time. These were people who had a long track record of understanding Washington and had real "hard news" chops. CNN was also interested in maintaining a real presence in Atlanta and in creating television talk show celebrities there. One of the first was Sandi Freeman with a show called *Freeman Reports*. If you wanted to be a guest on her show, you had to fly to Atlanta to do it, because the current era of live broadcasts done remotely was in its technical infancy.

I was asked to be a guest, so CNN got me a flight and I got a haircut before flying south. Sandi's show was extraordinary by today's "say it all in 5 minutes" standard. She would have three guests on for the entire hour. With me were Karen McKay, who ran the Committee for a Free Afghanistan, and Phyllis Schlafly. The topics were all about women in the military. At the time I was the editor of the *Military Law Reporter*, that highly specialized publication sold mainly to the Department of Defense.

I remember little of the content of the show. As is often the case, the most interesting conversation occurred at dinner after the show was over when the three of us were dining at a fancy restaurant in Atlanta. When we sat down, Karen pulled out of her large handbag several copies of *Soldier of Fortune* magazine. "I bring these along everywhere I go," she said. I assumed this practice was to intimidate men she was dating but I didn't ask.

After checking in on information about people's families, I thought it was time to probe into Phyllis' psyche. "Phyllis, don't you think there are some 'traditional' roles for men and women that are harmful to our culture?" I was shocked when she responded, "Maybe." She then explained that it was too dangerous to start unraveling them. "When it comes to family, there are some important roles for the husband and the wife."

"Like what?"

Her response was, "Like taking out the garbage."

I was genuinely confused by this because I really wasn't sure which party should take out the garbage. So, I asked and she said, as if I was a nitwit not to know, "The man of course."

"Why?"

"Because there might be animals outside at the can."

Schafly lived in Alton, Illinois, a Chicago suburb, and I could not imagine what creatures she was talking about short of escaped lions from a circus. Did she think the common animals of suburban America, like raccoons or squirrels, posed a unique threat to American women? I decided to terminate that piece of the conversation. The whole epicurean experience lasted about an hour and a half.

A few years later, as discussed earlier, I was asked to debate Phyllis at that convention of the American Association of School Administrators in Washington on morality in public schools. My main point was that what was said by teachers and administrators was far less important than how those officials treated the students in their care. Phyllis was a longtime critic of public schools, in part because there was no religious education there. She said teachers' unions were bloated reservoirs of incompetent people, and that schools taught reading using the "look-see" method instead of phonics. Those were common criticisms by rightwing critics at this time.

Imagine my surprise after these experiences with her at finding Phyllis at an organizing meeting of a coalition to stop the call for a new constitutional convention. Many people on the left and the right believed that it was essential to convene a second constitutional convention to make clearer what rights were guaranteed by the document. The ACLU, for whom I had previously worked, opposed the idea, in no small measure because it feared that people on the political and religious right would end up being able to organize enough people to take over any convention and ban abortion and birth control, regulate sexual material, explicitly guarantee private ownership of all kinds of guns, and reduce voting rights. People on the right like Phyllis worried that it was the left that would seize a new convention and propose legitimizing reproductive choice, making voting easier, and (in Phyllis' case) include an "Equal Rights Amendment."

Phyllis' landmark achievement had been to derail passage of the ERA when it was a hair's breadth away from being ratified by the two-thirds of state legislatures required to add it to the Constitution. Whenever I would run into her in the later years of her life, she'd say something like, "Well, Barry, at least you were on the correct side of the new constitutional convention debate."

Phyllis was the heart and soul of the anti-feminist movement, but she was not necessarily its best advocate. There were plenty of other women who did a better job at making the case for the conservative agenda. At one time or another I debated almost all of them.

Andrea Sheldon was the daughter of the late Lou Sheldon, founder of the Traditional Values Coalition in California, a group opposed to every single thing I ever stood for. That Coalition was savvy enough to gain a following well beyond California and eventually set up an office in Washington, DC. Andrea didn't look like a prudish person, or a traditional conservative. She was delighted to have photographs of her in a leopard skin mini skirt. She drove a red sportscar with a "CA GAL" license plate, and she had a sense of humor.

How funny was she? When Chris Matthews was to begin his *Hardball* television show on MSNBC, the network wanted him to tape a run-through the night before the show was to start airing. His producer thought it would be great to have him host a debate between Andrea and me to kick things off. Immediately before the taping, Chris said, "I hope we can keep this lively."

Andrea just smiled and quipped, "It will be because Barry is my ex-husband."

I was on Chris' show many times after that but I never again saw him speechless.

He started the show by noting that he was eager to have this opening debate. "I just learned something that might make it even more intense," he added. At the break, she noted that she was just joking about our prior marital state, and he seemed genuinely relieved to learn that. This somewhat silly joke she repeated on many other occasions—at one Voice of America taping she asked if a student who was there for a tour would mind sitting on a bench between us because, "He is my ex-husband and I don't want to be close to him." The student may never have recovered from that shock.

Andrea eventually married a man named James Lafferty and gradually seemed to retire from the advocacy business. She and her husband did get into a nasty dispute with her father some years before he died. I am assuming she never mentioned to James her previous (fake) relationship.

I had only one public encounter with Ann Coulter, at the Regent University Clash of the Titans. She certainly wasn't a fan of mine before or after. In her obituary for Jerry Falwell, she said the only disagreement she had with him was when he laid blame for the attacks of September 11 on various groups including gays and feminists but did not personally name Senator Edward Kennedy and Barry Lynn as the precipitating cause. Then, after Hurricane Katrina (which she did not blame on me), she noted that "Barry Lynn's church" (the United Church of Christ in which I am an ordained minister) probably "didn't do much" for the victims. True to her journalistic scholarship she hadn't looked into this, or she would have discovered that the United Church of Christ had given $4.4 million in disaster relief and had even organized trips to New Orleans for volunteers to help the victims in person.

In late summer 2009, I was checking my email one morning and found that a number of people had forwarded me her most recent column. I wondered why and thought maybe she had had a miraculous conversion to the cause of church/state separation. Alas, no.

Ann had written a column about people who hate their own kind—as in Southerners who concede the racism of their area, Vietnam veterans who talk about atrocities they witnessed, and ministers (to be precise, one) who are anti-religion. She continued that I was not only *not* a true minister, but that I wasn't even a Christian. She was not suggesting I had violated some Scriptural tenet or didn't accept some doctrine. She was saying I was not Christian, but Jewish: "The first person to post Barry Lynn's bar mitzvah photos or birth certificate (mazel tov!) wins a free copy of my latest book."

How does one respond to this? I chose to do a blog about it featuring a photo of a birth certificate and my parents and me at a New Jersey beach. The birth certificate was an ancient one from Cameroon that somebody on the AU staff had found in the trash. I blurred the actual name of the holder and printed in bold letters, "BARRY WILLIAM LYNN." The beach photo was a phony "photoshopped" picture of two large-headed space aliens holding their "son," an alien with my face superimposed. I noted in the blog that this was written simply to correct her misinformation because I would not want to sully her scholarly reputation. This was a joke also because her recent books on Joe McCarthy and evolution had been savaged by historians *and* scientists for their loopy conclusions and ridiculous "evidence." I got no response and certainly didn't get that free book she had promised. I am pretty certain I never saw her again.

Michelle Malkin is a syndicated columnist who often made Ann Coulter seem like Shirley Temple in her youth. I only had two brief encounters with her. The first was in the Green Room of Fox News one Saturday night. I had never met her, but she seemed curious about what I was there to talk about. I thought I'd have a little fun so I answered, "I'm here to explain why 'The Simpsons' depicts the ideal American family." She seemed horrified, so I admitted that I was there to talk about the separation of church and state.

Then in 2009, she wrote a column in which she criticized the Hawaii Senate for passing a resolution declaring Islam Day. She mentioned that only one legislator had voted against it on grounds that it violated separation of church and state. Malkin railed, "Where is Barry Lynn?" Not being everywhere in the nation at the same time, I'll admit I did not know this resolution had been passed but agreed that this action, like national days of prayer, was totally inappropriate. I would have given her a scoop of me dissing the day if she had just called. Americans United is in the phonebook and I have never had a personal unlisted telephone number. I never heard from her after that. Perhaps consistency in my viewpoint just bothered her.

In 2006, I had a chance to chat on the radio with Katharine DeBrecht, who was pretty upset with the kind of books she was hearing about in school libraries. She decided to write her own books for young people including such gems as *Help! Mom! There Are Liberals Under My Bed!* and the equally provocative, *Help! Mom! Hollywood's In My Hamper!* Just to clarify, the latter book has "liberal" celebrities who are modeled after Britney Spears and Madonna appearing in the closet of two sisters and who convince the sisters to spend their babysitting money on fashion items that turn out to be garish and uncomfortable.

When our *Cultureshocks* producer tracked her down, she was eager to join me on air. I had to remind her that some of the very things that happen in her books are remarkably similar to incidents in other books widely attacked by her fellow social conservatives. Case in point: a boy puts a worm in a girl's purse which seems to mirror a widely criticized volume in which a boy puts a slug in his father's pajamas. My gentle chiding went on. In her book when those girls conclude that their expensive clothing was a waste of money, they burn the items. I told her it would be a better message if they had given them to a charity that runs a thrift store. My broader point was that some rightwing advocacy groups get a tad too upset regarding the impact of specific images on children (inappropriate use of icky invertebrates) and too facile in figuring out how to communicate proper values in print. She actually seemed to enjoy the appearance, despite my teasing.

There were many leaders of actual feminist organizations I worked closely with in Washington. I was in awe of Feminist Majority leader Eleanor Smeal for at least a decade before I had a chance to meet her. My previous contact with her had been interviewing her on various radio shows I had done and watching her on television. As Americans United was nudged to get more directly involved in issues of reproductive justice, I would run into her at coalition meetings. I thought her brand of commitment and clarity of vision—mixed with an edginess that was so sharp—was mesmerizing.

By 2005, when John Roberts was nominated to be Chief Justice of the Supreme Court, the "go to" organization for responses to Supreme Court nominations was People for The American Way, the group founded by television producer and liberal activist Norman Lear. Running the organization was Ralph Neas, a former aide to Senator Edward Brooke of Massachusetts. He had joined People For just before the Supreme Court nomination of Robert Bork and was widely credited by the press with derailing Bork's nomination by exposing his past extremist views. Bork's nomination to the Court was defeated 58-42 on October 23, 1987, because of the research that exposed his past extremist views, producing a new verb— "borked." Because the Roberts nomination was announced late in the afternoon, television networks all wanted to get Ralph's take on the nominee. Neas had very little to say that evening but promised a full report on the nomination in the near future.

This response did not sit well with some others who had been major players in the effort to defeat Bork, including Ellie Smeal, then President of the National Organization for Women; Sammie Moshenberg, the veteran Washington representative for the National Council of Jewish Women; and many reproductive rights leaders. It didn't sit well with me, either. I joined these feminists in weekly sessions about how to handle the Roberts nomination without including People for the American Way.

For me, John Roberts was obviously a terrible choice. My only personal encounter with him had been a debate on CNN when he was in private legal practice and had been a staunch advocate for school vouchers for private schools.

Ellie was the leader of our group of early advocates for his defeat. Eventually when the People For report on Roberts was issued and called for Roberts' rejection, our group merged with People For in our member advocacy and public commentary. There were no "smoking guns" in Roberts' past and his nomination was approved on a 72-22 vote with half of the Democrats supporting him, concluding that he was a moderate.

I was always honored when Ellie helped get me invited to participate as a speaker at major events. At her annual conferences, I was given the remarkable opportunity to share the stage with feminist leaders like Gloria Steinem; Mavis Leno, spouse of the popular late night NBC show host; and reproductive rights advocate Sandra Fluke, who became a nationally known leader when, as a student at Georgetown University Law Center, she was denied coverage for birth control and then labeled a slut by rightwing talk show host Rush Limbaugh.

At a 2015 forum on "Women, Money and Power," I was the last speaker on a morning panel and had a chance to do two things that made my day. First, I was able to use the word "bullshit" in my speech, claiming that I had never heard the word before a few days earlier when Senator Rick Santorum had used it in a testy interview with *The New York Times.* Later in my speech, I held up a black T-shirt with the words "This is What a Feminist Looks Like" emblazoned on the front.

One year later, in 2016, when I spoke at a Feminist Majority conference, I said I was supportive of three-quarters of Donald Trump's Presidential platform, which produced loud gasps and grew even louder when I added, "and I have a hat to prove it." I pulled out an iconic red Trump hat with a Band-Aid over the word "Again." The gasps ceased when I said, "The idea that America was great at some Golden Era of the past is nonsense. People like us have worked and litigated and marched and agitated to make America great, but we have never actually gotten there."

I repeated this same message at a NOW conference a few months before the 2016 election and to the Leadership Conference on Civil and Human Rights annual dinner. My friend Wade Henderson asked me to fill in with that invocation when an African American Baptist preacher had to cancel at the last minute. I was discouraged that Secretary Hillary Clinton's response to Trump's "Make America Great Again" motto was "We are great already." I didn't think so.

Ellie invited me to a post-election event at her apartment in 2016. I went fully expecting to join in the massive celebration for the election of the first woman President. Barely inside the door, she motioned for me to join her in a corner and said, "Things are not looking good." She was in touch with hundreds of women who were observing polling places in key states and the voters didn't "look like our folks." It was a disheartening event, to be followed by an even more upsetting party.

By the time I got back to our Maryland neighborhood, it was clear that Secretary Clinton was going to lose Florida, Pennsylvania, North Carolina—even Wisconsin and Michigan. She might be ahead in the popular vote (nearly three million ahead when all the votes were counted) but she would lose in the Electoral College.

It was a grim, sleepless night for many of us. I had planned to have everyone at Americans United get the next day off. Instead, we went to work and shared our grief at a staff meeting. That was a terrible depressing day. We had high hopes for a responsive Supreme Court, a spirited defense of LGBTQ+ rights, and so much more. All dashed.

The National Organization for Women has always been one of my favorite advocacy groups. It was founded by Betty Friedan, the author of *The Feminine Mystique*, (1963) a groundbreaking analysis of inequality. Many of NOW's future presidents became my friends, including Gloria Steinem. She used to say when we'd run into each other, "I love the name of your group because it says exactly what you stand for." I worked with Kim Gandy, who was instrumental in the creation of the March for Women's Lives in 2014, Terry O'Neill, and Toni Van Pelt, who I first knew when she ran a Florida chapter of Americans United for the Separation of Church and State.

Before Cecile Richards became the President of Planned Parenthood, she had created and run the Texas Freedom Network out of Austin, Texas. It was a beautiful model of how to organize clergy and secularists to return common sense to a state that was sinking into ultra-conservatism. Cecile's mother had been the last progressive Democratic governor of the state, Ann Richards. Richards' wonderful comments on life and politics were so clever that they formed the basis for a play about her life.

Molly Ivins was a longtime columnist and cultural critic in Texas, and she held legendary first Friday of the month parties. On a visit to Austin in 2000, I was invited to join the head of the Texas Freedom Network, Samantha Smoot, attending that event. Molly always said if you were an attendee with a friend in town, you should bring the friend. There was a catch, though: attendees were expected to compose a joke, limerick, song, or poem and deliver it before everyone. Deciding that a poem was the way to go and given that I had spent seven-and-a-half-hours on airplanes to get to Austin, I had plenty of time to come up with one. With another half hour it would have been as long as "Beowulf."

The subject I chose was the tale of Janet Reno, then Attorney General, and her decision to return a young boy named Elian Gonzalez to his father in Cuba, something opposed by most Cuban Americans who were appalled by the decision. Six stanzas of doggerel poetry which used the phrase "love child" several times went over quite well. I don't have a copy of the poem, considering that it was a tad risqué for publication. Many years later, though, I was giving an award to Kathy Miller, the Texas Freedom Network's current director. She reminded me she had been at Molly's party that night and brought up my poem. Thankfully she didn't have a transcript or recording of it.

IN CLOSING

Feminism for me was the single most important ideology in modern history. It was responsible for a dramatic increase in women seeking and winning electoral office and for shaping the futures of women throughout this country and the world. It shifted the culture as well.

When I would take my daughter Christina to movies, we saw few positive women role models. Now, major roles for women in films are common, no longer housewife stereotypes but including women in most professions. Women are now directors, producers, writers, and camera operators. Women comedians and songwriters have begun to thrive. *Captain Marvel* is a woman and women's stories are often taken seriously. The week after the 2022 Bans Off Our Bodies march, I saw a French film called *Happening*, a brilliant and graphic depiction of the horrors faced by a young woman in 1940's France when contraception and abortion were outlawed. We don't need to wonder what will happen with *Roe v. Wade* overturned or speculate if things will get as bad as the future is depicted in Margaret Atwood's *The Handmaid's Tale.* We need only to listen to people over seventy who remember.

About the Author

Barry W. Lynn caused lots of good trouble. He worked in Washington from 1974 to 2017–first for the United Church of Christ (UCC), helping gain amnesty for Vietnam war resisters and trying to stop registration for the draft; then for the ACLU, defending the First Amendment and destroying the Meese Pornography Commission; and finally for Americans United for Separation of Church and State, doing battle with every Religious Right leader aiming to have government adopt their agendas. Lynn is an ordained minister in the UCC and a lawyer with membership in the Supreme Court Bar.

Go to Barry Lynn's website *https://barrywlynn.com* to see videos and where he's speaking.

Index

Symbols

A

B

L

M

P

Q

R